THE MISS GRAMMAR GUIDEBOOK

By
Karen Larsen, Ph.D.

Published by The Oregon State Bar
5200 S.W. Meadows Road
Lake Oswego, Oregon 97035

Editorial/production supervision
and interior design by Paul Nickell
Cover design by Bob Knowles
Manufactured in the United States of America

1 2 3 4 5 6 7 8 9 0

Library of Congress Cataloging in Publication Data

Larsen, Karen
   The Miss Grammar guidebook / Karen Larsen, Ph.D.
      p. cm.
   ISBN 1-879049-01-5
   Includes: bibliography; index.
   1. English language—Rhetoric. 2. English language—Grammar—
1950-   . 3. English language—Terms and phrases. I. Title.
PE1408.L37.M57   1994
808'.042-dc20

Library of Congress Catalog Card Number: 94-67937

To
Miss Timmerman,
who spent many years
making good work better

CONTENTS

ACKNOWLEDGMENTS

This guidebook came about because of the Oregon legal community's warm response to the persona of Miss Grammar, a response that never fails to surprise and delight me. Thank you, one and all.

I also wish to thank my own firm, Miller, Nash, Wiener, Hager & Carlsen, for its unflagging support; Paul Nickell, my cheerful OSB editor; and above all, Karen Magnuson, my legal editor, whose faithful attention to detail made the text as error-free as anyone could hope for. Angels could do no better.

—*Karen Larsen*

PREFACE

I came to Miller, Nash, Wiener, Hager & Carlsen in 1981, after a dozen years of defending my honor in college lecture halls.

"Miss Grammar," my alter ego, was born in 1983, when I began printing letters from staff and attorneys along with my replies in the firm's in-house newsletter. The Victorian lady has ruled much of my life ever since.

Seeking *Lebensraum* (or something), Miss G. began airing her multiple views in the Oregon State Bar *Bulletin* in June 1988; since then the column has also appeared regularly in California, Delaware, Hawaii, Iowa, New Mexico, Tennessee, and Washington and has been reprinted widely.

This book is a compilation of the most useful of the language tips that have appeared during the last five years; this is not a comprehensive introduction to or study of grammar, style, and usage—good handbooks abound, and the world probably doesn't need another one. This is simply a collection of the troublesome things that keep coming up in legal writing year after year. Both the *Bulletin* and I have been pestered regularly for copies of certain columns and for an indexed compilation—this, then, is our response to those requests.

Purely entertaining, hilarious material has been left out, and discussions that originally appeared as letters and answers have been edited to look as though Miss Grammar were talking to herself, something she does all the time anyway.

Even if you don't find your favorites in here, I hope you will find useful entries and helpful hints—and maybe a chuckle or two besides.

—Karen Larsen
Portland, Oregon 1994

THE
MISS GRAMMAR
GUIDEBOOK

CHERISHED NOTIONS

Most of us have our mental closets stuffed with misinformation gathered over the years—don't split an infinitive, don't end a sentence with a preposition, etc. If we remember nothing else of our English Composition 101, we remember those rules. Let's take a closer look at them.

The Split Infinitive

Fowler tells us:

> "The English-speaking world may be divided into (1) those who neither know nor care what a split infinitive is; (2) those who do not know, but care very much; (3) those who know and condemn; (4) those who know and approve; and (5) those who know and distinguish.
>
> "Those who neither know nor care are the vast majority, and are a happy folk, to be envied by most of the minority classes." H. W. Fowler, *A Dictionary of Modern English Usage* 579 (2d ed 1965).

It is a mistake to say "always" or "never" when discussing matters of grammar, and while we may say, generally, that we should not split the parts of an infinitive (that is, insert an adverb between *to* and the verb), there are times when splitting the infinitive is preferable to not splitting it. The key is that (1) the split must be made by only one or two words, and (2) the result must be idiomatic—it must sound like English spoken or written by a mature, intelligent native speaker of English.

> *Bad Split*: "Jones is the man to, whether you are a liberal, conservative, or moderate, vote for."
>
> *Good Split*: "I desire to so arrange my affairs that the merger will have little effect on me."
>
> *Good Split*: "Our object is to further improve trade relations."

Ordinarily it is good practice to keep the parts of the infinitive together. We should try the adverb before and after the verb to see whether one of those positions expresses our meaning before we decide to split the infinitive.

Split Infinitive Award

"Green, in his capacity as president, failed to and the defendant directors failed to require Green to, among other things, approve the loans and advances."

As Follows

Now and then someone asks, "Why isn't it *as follow*, instead of *as follows*, when a list of things (plural) is meant?"

This is a problem of subject-verb agreement with an *unexpressed* subject. Small wonder it causes difficulties.

Regardless of the number of the preceding noun, the established form is *as follows*: His reply was as follows (singular). The events scheduled today are as follows (plural).

Both take *as follows*, regardless of singular or plural, because the subject lies elsewhere: the subject of *follows* is generally construed as *it* unexpressed.

Preposition at End

Fowler speaks of the "cherished superstition that prepositions must be kept true to their name and placed before the word they govern in spite of the incurable English instinct for putting them late." That worthy grammarian takes the position that the old boys (e.g., Dryden and Gibbon) were "overpowered by notions of correctness derived from Latin standards" and have saddled us with this irksome prohibition.

Common sense and a good ear confirm what Fowler says— English has remarkable freedom in placement of its prepositions:

> "It was the strangest thing I had ever heard of."
> "The Board seized every property it could get its hands on."
> "Faith is what we live by."

Sir Winston Churchill, mildly nettled by the old prohibition, declared, "This is the sort of English up with which I will not put."

It is a painful thing to find that a familiar rule hugged to one's bosom all one's life is not venerated by the world at large—further, one is told that one is just plain wrong. Miss Grammar can only sympathize. She still remembers her mortification at learning (in college!) that *misled* is not pronounced my-zuld.

Can You Top This?

B. B. Lyon, of Portland, Oregon, sends this example of a sentence ending in prepositions:

A certain man went upstairs each night to read his son a bedtime story. The boy didn't like the book his father had chosen. One night when he saw his father walk in with the same old book, he said, "What are you always bringing that book I don't want to be read to out of up for?!"

2

COMMAS

Superfluous Comma With *That*

Basically, the rule is that two commas are needed to set off an *interrupting* dependent clause:

> "He said that, as you may already know, he was planning to take early retirement."

> "They told me that, just as a suggestion, I should file early."

Note: Sentences like these are rare; generally speaking, be very cautious about inserting a comma after *that*.

No comma precedes a dependent clause if it is introductory, but many people routinely and mistakenly put a comma after *that*:

> "Doctors will tell you that, when a child is tired and pale, the cause is often lack of nutritious food."

In other words, a comma follows only the dependent clause, just as if the sentence began with the word *when*. Placing a comma after *that* is interrupting and distracting.

In the following typical sentences culled from legal documents, the commas after *that* are *unnecessary* and *undesirable*:

> "Marshall stated that, in any memo arguing for the opposite, the attorney should not simply cite case holdings."

> "He simply told the judge at the beginning of the argument that, if the judge is not inclined to make the award, he would like to put on an expert witness."

> "It follows that, if the trial judge applied the old rule rather than the new, the ruling by the trial court was improper."

> "Plaintiff testified that, when he started to cross the street, he saw defendant's car about 250 feet to the south."

> "The Supreme Court recognized that, while the general rule is applicable here, it may not apply if the union refuses to press its claim."

The Serial Comma

The serial comma is used to separate items in a series. Problems arise when we must decide whether to use a comma before the conjunction. If we use the final comma, the last two items in the series may be considered separately, not in combination. The omission of this final comma can cause confusion:

> "He turned over all his holdings, houses and lands."

In that sentence, *houses* and *lands* might be construed as explaining the word *holdings*. But with a comma preceding *and*, three distinct elements become immediately evident: holdings and houses and lands. *The Grammatical Lawyer* states that

> "some writers prefer to omit it. And yet its omission can cause confusion, even misunderstanding, whereas its presence never does. * * *
>
> * * *

"Since serial commas aid clarity, the better practice is to use them regularly. They will not harm a sentence—may even help it." Morton S. Freeman, *The Grammatical Lawyer* 91 (1979).

Miss Grammar agrees. The State of Oregon in its statutes, however, does not use the final comma unless there is danger of misreading. Many conservative firms use the final serial comma, but some prefer to follow journalistic style and omit it. Because consistency is so important, those who use the final comma have the advantage—once the decision is made, that comma will always appear. Those who use it only when there is the possibility of misreading must make the decision repeatedly and must risk being thought inconsistent.

For a series in a company name, always follow the style preferred by the particular firm.

Crawford, Crawford & Newton
Hart Schaffner & Marx

If you do not have the company's letterhead or some other reliable resource at hand, follow the standard rule on commas in a series.

3

HYPHENS

Those lucky Germans! They can write words like *Sonntagnachmittagsspaziergang* with neither space nor hyphen, but in English we are stuck with hyphens.

Reference manuals, like Gregg's seventh edition, contain dozens of pages of detailed information on the use of hyphens, much of which is seemingly contradictory and nearly all of which is impossible to remember. If her readers will forgive her for glossing over a difficult area, Miss Grammar will present a few very simple remarks about hyphens.

1. Authorities do not agree on hyphen rules. Style is continually changing: many words that used to be hyphenated are now written as one word or as two separate words.

2. Hyphens act as ropes to tie together words that might otherwise drift apart and render an incorrect meaning:

> "There were no smoking rooms for the staff."
> "There were no-smoking rooms for the staff."

3. Some compounds are so familiar that there is no longer any danger of their drifting around:

> real estate agent
> income tax return
> work product doctrine
> high school diploma
> public relations adviser

4. A good, current dictionary may be your best guide.

We need to be aware that the words change in appearance as they change parts of speech, too. It is not possible to declare that a verb-based compound is always hyphenated. A familiar pattern in which we have a verb, then an adjective, and finally a noun stemming from that verb is this:

> **Verb:** Two words. "The contractor will pick up the lumber on Monday."
>
> **Adjective:** Hyphenated or one word—check dictionary. "We played a pickup game of baseball."
>
> **Noun:** One word. "The Jensen Company never made the pickup."

This process is extremely idiosyncratic. Observe the contrariness of *date stamp*. As a noun it is two words, and as a verb it is hyphenated!

> "Hand me that date stamp, Fred, and I'll date-stamp the package."

Similarly, we may not say that "ly" words are never hyphenated, as we are tempted to do. It is true that "wholly owned subsidiary" is not hyphenated, but "motherly-looking woman" is. The former is an adverb-participle compound; the latter is an adjective-participle compound.

Miss Grammar is not telling you this to be vexatious; rather, in matters of grammar as in domestic quarrels, it is wise to refrain from making statements containing "always" and "never."

The Well-Tempered Hyphen

Well needs a hyphen if it accompanies a past participle that precedes a noun:

> "That was a well-directed operation."
> "She is a well-dressed woman."

But when *well* and the participle follow a verb, *well* is *not* hyphenated if those two words can sensibly be reversed:

> "The operation was planned well."
> "The woman is dressed well."

Thus:

> "The operation was well planned."
> "The woman is well dressed."

If the sense of the sentence is affected, however, a hyphen should be used. For example, it makes no sense to say:

> "The judge was read well," or
> "The premise was founded well,"

so we would use hyphens:

> "The judge was well-read."
> "The premise was well-founded."

To simplify, let us think of it in this way: If the term is "strong" and can stand on its own even when reversed, it does not need the hyphen to brace it. But if it wobbles when reversed, it is "weak" and needs to be shored up with a hyphen.

4

Inclusive Language

Miss Grammar catches an occasional rap on the knuckles, even though she *never* deserves it, but she was once surprised to find herself being chastised for ignoring *women* in her column, specifically by excluding women in the examples she uses. Her defense? The examples usually illustrate some gaffe or other, and she likes to hang gaffes on the men. [There was not a word of truth in that, but it made a fine excuse.] Her critic wasn't having any of *that*, however—the impression remained the same: that only men *did* things.

Therefore, operating under the principle that repentance, like charity, begins at home, Miss Grammar here offers some guidelines for equal treatment of the sexes (in language) and vows to follow her own instruction.

Parallel descriptions and terms should be used for men and women:

> *Not:* James Turner is an orthopedic surgeon, and his wife, Marie, is a vibrant blonde.
>
> *Better:* James Turner is an orthopedic surgeon, and his wife, Marie, is a deputy district attorney.

Or: James Turner is a striking redhead, and his wife, Marie, is a vibrant blonde.

Not: the men and the ladies
Better: the gentlemen and the ladies
Or: the men and the women

Not: the men and the wives
Better: the husbands and the wives

Not: Harold Jones and Millie
Better: Harold Jones and Millie Edwards

Avoid "feminine" words and diminutive word forms: authoress, Jewess, aviatrix, litigatrix, usherette, etc. [Miss G. notes that a title like *princess* or *countess* is acceptable, but *actress* is rapidly giving way to *actor* for both sexes, except for Academy Award purposes. Sometimes it seems we will be stuck forever with *executrix, testatrix, conciliatrix,* etc.]

Drop sex-identifying modifiers whenever possible. Try to avoid giving the impression that only men do certain jobs and only women do certain others. Especially annoying is the use of *lady* as a modifier.

Avoid:

> male nurse
> lady lawyer
> woman driver
> male secretary
> lady truck driver

If you truly need to specify sex, use *male* or *female* [but you'd better have a good reason].

"Melanie Pierce was this university's first female microscopist."

"The male secretaries in our firm are paid exactly what the female secretaries are paid."

Include women as participants. Nouns should not be used as though they applied only to men:

Not: Many lawyers put in so many hours that they neglect their wives and children.

Better: Many lawyers put in so many hours that they neglect their families.

Not: Ranchers in eastern Oregon often take their wives and children to cattle auctions.

Better: Ranchers in eastern Oregon often attend cattle auctions with their families.

Not: Married students will have to pay extra for their wives' dinners.

Better: Married students will have to pay extra for their spouses' dinners.

Watch out for the word *man* when something else would work as well.

NO	*YES*
mankind	human beings, human race, people, humanity, humankind
cavemen	cave people
early man	early people, primitive people
the best man for the job	the best person
manmade	handmade, manufactured, synthetic
manpower	workers, work force
man-hours	hours of work, worker hours
statesman	official, public servant

[*Fire fighter, mail carrier, salesperson*, etc., are so popular now that they really do not need to be listed.]

Don't lean too heavily on the generic singular *he*.

Because English lacks a singular gender-free pronoun for persons, it has been customary to use (a) *he* as a generic pronoun ("he who hesitates is lost"), (b) *he or she*, or (c) increasingly, *they*—unacceptable to literate folk ("If you find a clerk to help you, make sure they take this cover off before they try to fix the connection").

Sometimes the best thing to do is cast the sentence in the plural.

> *Not*: The average employee likes to see earned vacation time on his paycheck.
>
> *Better*: Most employees like to see earned vacation time on their paychecks.

Don't flirt with typographical manipulation.

Writing *he/she, s/he, she/he* will not help anyone—readers hear words in their heads even if they read silently to themselves, and these things are as hard to say as they are to look at.

5

ME, MYSELF, AND OTHER PRONOUNS

When Is It *I* and When Is It *Me*?

Having been taught when we were little *never* to say "Jim and me are going to the movies," we hear our mothers' voices over and over, saying, "Jim and *I*. Jim and *I*!" Thus we lapse into errors like these:

> "Judge Holman called the meeting for the benefit of Jim and I."

> "Merrill Lynch sent over these new prospectuses for Jim and I."

> "At the stockholders' meeting, the chairman of the board sat beside she and I."

Most certainly we would never say "sat beside I" or "sat beside she," but make it compound and we seem to lose all sense of grammatical bearing. At the extreme, this disorientation will result in such phenomenal grammatical distortions as "Betty and I's office."

The helpful hint, of course, as implied above, is to separate the pronoun parts of the sentence and see how each sounds alone.

If we are tempted to say, "Her and they have objected to that approach," take the sentence apart. There is nothing wrong with "They have objected," but there is definitely something askew in "Her [has] objected."

Hypercorrectivity

This ailment afflicts panicky types who wish fervently to be correct in their use of English, so fervently that they overcorrect their driving, running their vehicles onto the grammatical curb and sometimes through a plate-glass window. Observe:

> "Just between you and I."
> [Should be "me"; the object of a preposition.]
>
> "This is our and they's only option."
> [Should be "our and their." If that sounds clumsy, recast: "We share this option," or something similar.]

Although not an example of confused subject/object, this common error is a fine specimen of hypercorrectivity at work:

> "I feel very badly about it."
> [Should be *bad*; *feel* is a verb of the senses, followed in most cases by adjectives. Ice cream tastes *good*, not *well*.]

Who/Whom

The use of *who* and *whom*, also part of the subject/object problem, confuses many people, even to the extent that some have given up altogether and use only *who*. Some grammarians say that *whom* is in the process of passing from the language, and at some future time the word *whom* may indeed become obsolete, but we may not throw it out now just because of that possibility.

We are not likely to make a mistake with the object of a preposition: "He is one of those judges about whom we know nothing."

Another hint may help to distinguish between *who* and *whom*: If you can substitute *him*, say *whom*. Match up the m's. If you must guess and have waxed desperate, choose *who*. Unless you're absolutely sure of yourself with *whom* and *whomever*, use *who* or recast the sentence. That's one of the most attractive things about English—there are always several correct ways to say something. Recasting is not cheating, no matter what our earliest teachers told us. Listen to Miss Grammar.

Myself

Myself is frequently employed by those who think *me* has a low-down, nongrammatical ring.

Myself is used as an intensive pronoun ("I myself have no intention of going") and a reflexive pronoun ("I cut myself in three places").

Myself is not a replacement for *I* or *me*. In each of these examples, the correct pronoun is in brackets.

> "Mr. Martin and myself [I] are pleased to have received your invitation."
>
> "He confided in Hayden as well as in myself [me]."
>
> "The conference will be attended by Jay Jones, Harriet Tibbs, and myself [me]."

If in doubt, separate *myself* from the rest of the sentence and read it with the verb ("please call myself"; "please call me").

If there is a rule, it is that *myself* should not be used in any construction in which *I* or *me* could be used.

A Note on *Myself*

If you are still having trouble, try it another way:

Generally, if you haven't said *I*, you can't say *myself*; if you haven't said *she*, you can't say *herself*, and so on.

> "I will be very happy to see that myself."
>
> "She never allows herself to be that wild."

No problem. These are correct usages. We may not say:

> "When you are in town, give my secretary or myself a call."
>
> "We will let herself decide that."
> ["We will let *her* decide that *herself*" is correct because the pronoun is used as an intensive.]

ONCE AGAIN, don't use *myself* if you have not used *I*.

Correct:

> "I myself have no intention of reading this."
>
> "I can fool myself only so many times."
>
> "I bruised myself when I fell."

Incorrect:

> "The meeting will be attended by Hopkins and myself [me]."
> [One more time: the word *I* does not precede *myself*; therefore, I may not use *myself*.]
>
> "Please direct the reply to Ross, Gilbert, and myself [me]."
>
> "Do you have something prepared especially for them and myself [me]?"

6

MISPLACED ELEMENTS

Direct Object

Miss Grammar has noticed two recurrent oddities in lawyers' writing. Both have to do with misplaced elements in the sentence. The first is a misplacing of the direct object:

> "The trustees will have at their disposal when such amendment is made financial data."
> [This is like saying, "The boys will see when vacation begins a movie" or "Toss the horse over the fence some hay."]

> "There is no authority which requires Good Hope Hospital to produce for inspection by a third person Mr. Brown's confidential medical records."

The syntax here is more German than English, satirized in the once-popular song "Throw Mama From the Train a Kiss."

A better version of the sentence:

> "There is no authority that requires Good Hope Hospital to produce Mr. Brown's confidential medical records for inspection by a third person."

19

Now the direct object is where it belongs: near its verb.

The second pattern of misplacement has to do with the undesirable splitting of a predicate adjective from its verb, as seen in this sentence:

> "Thus, suits to challenge Harbor's personal contracts are, by the express terms of the statute, subject to challenge in this court."

Are is far removed from its complement, *subject*. Much better is the following:

> "Thus, by the express terms of the statute, suits to challenge Harbor's personal contracts are subject to challenge in this court."

Miss Grammar realizes that many things are written under pressure and in haste and with that in mind urges the old adage, "Compose in haste, revise at leisure."

Position of Adverb

What is the normal place of an adverb used with a compound verb?

> "We also *already have met* with the appropriate support staff."

Should the two parts of the verb stay together; should the modifiers precede or follow the whole verb? Should the adverb split up the happy pair?

First of all, a compound verb is a verb made up of an auxiliary (or more than one) and an infinitive (without *to*) or participle:

  — *will* (auxiliary) *see* (infinitive)

  — *has* (auxiliary) *spoken* (participle)

The normal place for the adverb when used with a compound verb is between the auxiliary and the rest of the verb. Thus, "have already met," not "already have met." *See* H. W. Fowler, *A Dictionary of Modern English Usage* 464 (2d ed 1965).

Some people harbor a deep suspicion of dividing compound verbs, which probably is connected to the prohibition against splitting infinitives.

Only

Perhaps the most frequently misplaced modifier is *only*. Because in informal, spoken English we tend to put *only* next to the verb ("But I only *had* two pieces!"), we are tempted to do so in formal, written English too, as in these two examples:

> *Not:* The New York courts have only applied the continuous representation theory to the three-year statute of limitations.
>
> *Better:* The New York courts have applied the continuous representation theory only to the three-year statute of limitations.
>
> *Not:* The provisions of the trust only allowed the decedent-grantor to exercise the removal power once.
>
> *Better:* The provisions of the trust allowed the decedent-grantor to exercise the removal power only once.

Because lawyers, more than any other group of writers, must anticipate the bad-faith reader, it is especially important to place modifiers close to the words they modify.

7

ODDITIES

The The Dalles?

David DeHart, of Miller Insurance, draws this to Miss Grammar's attention: Because the name of The Dalles includes *The* in its full name, must the definite article be repeated at times?

> "Of the Portland police officers present, 42 declined to vote."

Hence:

> "Of the The Dalles police officers present, two declined to speak."

Miss Grammar doesn't know what to think of that. In her geographical dictionary[1] she finds only two entries under *The*: The Dalles and The Hague. These two names also appear in William A. Sabin, *The Gregg Reference Manual* ¶ 336 (7th ed 1992), in

---

[1] This dictionary also lists an alternate name for The Dalles: "Dalles City."

which the reader is told to capitalize *The* when it is part of a place name.

Relatedly: When Miss Grammar lived in the Salinas Valley some years ago, she noticed that when King City was mentioned in a legal description, it was called "the City of King," not "the City of King City." Miss Grammar thinks that might be incorrect, or at least inconsistent. Would we speak of the City of Oregon or the City of Oregon City?

Vex the Proofreader

This sentence contains frequently misspelled words:

> "On the rococo threshold of a cemetery sat a harassed physician and an embarrassed psychiatrist, picnicking on a desiccated apple with mayonnaise and gazing at the symmetry of a fuchsia with unparalleled ecstasy, when the physician said, 'I see by your vermilion moccasins that you are an impostor, but in this pavilion that's not a sacrilege.'"

Inversion: Poetic or Political

While waiting for a bus recently and brooding quietly on matters grammatical, Miss Grammar chanced to notice the title of a book that a young woman was reading: *When Comes the Spring*. No question mark, which somehow made it worse. At least "When comes the spring?" (or better yet, "when comes the bus?") would have had some substance.

The book was a romance, and its title had been crafted to reflect that—*When the Spring Comes* would not sound as "special," just as "he roamed the wide world over" has its own romantic fragrance, also due in part to inversion.

What we want to watch out for is the stylistic or poetic inversion creeping into our formal writing. It is one thing for

President Kennedy to *say* "Ask not what your country can do for you" (and some people say he *barely* got away with that) and quite another for us to *write* "it matters not" in a memorandum. Even this stylistic inversion is probably to be avoided: "Compromise he totally abhorred." When comes the inversion, then screams Miss Grammar.

Holding Harmless

Even though we speak of a "hold harmless" agreement, we must not hesitate to put the two words asunder if a direct object comes along. This sentence sounds decidedly peculiar:

> "Federal Depositors will also agree to defend, indemnify, and hold harmless Jones from all such claims, demands, causes of action, or orders."

> *Better*: "Federal Depositors will also agree to defend, indemnify, and hold Jones harmless from all such claims, demands, causes of action, or orders."

Window, or Window of Opportunity

This is being used too often and used inappropriately. Not every period equals a "window." The expression comes from a reference to the exact time and directional limits governing the launching of a rocket to achieve a certain orbit or destination, which may be pictured as a *window* through which the rocket must be shot. A 30-day application period is just that, not a "window" of any kind.

Mixed Metaphors and Dangling Modifiers

Lawyers like to use metaphors; Miss G. likes them too, but straight up, not mixed.

A metaphor is a figure of speech: "The chairman has his head in the sand." If two such figures are incongruously mixed, we have a nonsensical and often amusing combination: "Playing with fire can get a person into deep water."

Although any misplaced word, phrase, or clause can be said to dangle, the term *dangling* is applied primarily to verbal phrases that do not refer clearly and logically to another word or phrase in the sentence. Often there is an "ing" word at the beginning of the sentence followed eventually by a comma; the noun or pronoun that comes next is seen as the thing doing the action of the "ing" word. Observe: "Having broken both its front legs, they carried the dog to the veterinarian." Animal cruelty, to be sure.

To correct a dangling modifier, either rearrange the words in the sentence to make the modifier refer clearly to the right word or add words to make the meaning clear and logical.

Better: "Having broken both its front legs, the dog was carried to the veterinarian."

Pay special attention to a sentence that begins with a phrase containing a participle followed by a comma, as Miss Grammar has laboriously pointed out, because the next noun or pronoun will grammatically be the subject, logic be hanged, as in:

> "Upon entering the room, the lamp fell over."
>
> "Walking in from the darkness, a dazzling-white, lifelike statue of Lincoln greets you."

And Miss Grammar's own favorite, although more in the nature of a misplaced modifier:

> "Nailed to the fence, Bobby saw a 'No Trespassing' sign."

Intrusive Phrases and Clauses

A vocalized pause is a noise made by a speaker to fill in what would otherwise be what the speaker perceives as an embarrassing silence. The all-time classic is *uh*. Also popular are *y'know*, *right*, *I mean*, and *see*. This aberration occurs in written English too—it may look like these examples:

> "You have, I trust, already seen the deposition."
>
> "The experts we have selected will, of course, be up to the task expected of them."
>
> "Here is the transcript which, as you know, was made yesterday."

Not one of these little throat-clearings is necessary; sprinkle enough of them in your letter and you will annoy your reader. Miss Grammar suspects that they are the natural offspring of the union of dictaphone and self-conscious attorney.

The most formal, deliberate kind of intrusive phrase appears in agreements:

> "The executor, after proper notification of all interested parties, will, pursuant to the provisions of the will, dispose of, by means of sealed bids, household items, including art works, silver, and antiques, whose sale will be conducted by, unless objectionable to the beneficiaries, a professional liquidation company."
>
> *Revised*: "Pursuant to [Under] the provisions of the will, the executor will notify all interested parties that the property is to be sold and will hire a professional liquidation company, unless the beneficiaries object. Household items, including works of art, silver, and antiques, will be sold by means of sealed bids."

A decided improvement, don't you think?

REDUNDANCIES

The Redundancy Department of Redundancy

A redundancy is an unnecessary and often unconscious repetition in the expression of ideas. Miss Grammar thinks redundancies may be the result of the writer's being too eager to make a point. Legal writing lends itself to repetition anyway, by virtue of its having inherited this sort of pattern:

> various and sundry
> unless and until
> save and except
> null and void
> each and every

Here are some common redundancies favored by many writers:

blue in color
rectangular in shape
new innovations
stray away from
revert back
young child
true fact
hollow tube
repeat it again
period of time
advance planning
mutually agree
resultant effect
invisible to the eye
few in number
consensus of opinion

POSSESSIVES

Names

Keith Bower, a kind and amusing gentleman from Redwood City, California, has asked Miss G. to comment on and give "rules" for forming possessives of proper nouns, specifically of names that end with an *s* sound.

Some of the "rules" are erratic, especially the one that asks us to determine how "most people would say it." A few years ago, Miss Grammar was working with a partner who had written about "Mr. Heinz' retirement." Miss Grammar suggested "Mr. Heinz's retirement" and confidently stated that most people would say it that way. The resourceful partner sent Miss G. to the inhabitants of six floors of a tall office building to determine exactly how "most people would say it." The consensus was "Heinz's." Gratifying though the experience was, it was also time-consuming—consequently Miss G. doesn't think much of that rule.

Some style manuals invite us to make up our own minds—we may write "Keats' poetry" or "Keats's poetry," as we wish. A grammatical blank check, Miss G. has learned, is generally more dismaying than delightful to its holder. Freedom can be frightening.

The *conservative* approach is to apply an apostrophe plus *s* to a proper noun ending with an *s* sound:

> "John Felix's [singular possessive] car was stolen, and so was his wife's station wagon."
>
> "The Felixes [simple plural] now walk everywhere."
>
> "The Felixes' [plural possessive] vehicles are long gone."
>
> "Margaret Lopez's election to state office was applauded."
>
> "The Lopezes are entertaining the Murphys tonight."
>
> "The Lopezes' Bombay kitten has taken Best of Show again."

Some Exceptions

If the addition of an extra syllable would make a name awkward to pronounce, we add the apostrophe only:

> Ms. Hodges' promotion
> Archimedes' principle
> Jesus' teachings
> Aristophanes' satirical comedies

Engaging and challenging are the proper nouns that end in a *silent s*. Some authorities urge us to write:

> Arkansas's mountains
> Des Moines's mayor
> Illinois's highways
> U.S. Marine Corps's history

Miss Grammar thinks this practice invites mispronunciation, and she recommends adding only the apostrophe.

Some proper nouns invite another kind of disaster when they go from singular to plural:

> John and Mary Wolf become the Wolfs, not the Wolves.
>
> Martin and Elizabeth Doberman become the Dobermans, not the Dobermen.

You may own two Mercedeses, but everyone will be happier if you refer to them as your two Mercedes-Benzes or do some other bit of recasting. Or trade them for two BMWs—no apostrophe.

Disturbing but Correct

Some nouns seem to pack a lot of *s* sounds, but we still need to add more:

> The business's failure (singular)
> The businesses' failure (plural)
> The witness's testimony (singular)
> The witnesses' testimony (plural)

Just Plain Disturbing

Lawyers have certain unusual forms of possessive that for one reason or another are firmly established. Among them:

> arm's length transaction (sometimes written with hyphen)
>
> attorney fees (sometimes attorneys' or attorney's fees)
>
> attorney's lien
>
> Congress' intent (U.S. Supreme Court preference)
>
> creditors' committee

Generally, the careful lawyer will consult Black's Law Dictionary for puzzling possessives of this sort. Customs vary from state to state too—as with *worker's* or *workers'* compensation. In Oregon, *Veterans' Affairs* at the state level has an apostrophe, but at the federal level it does not—it's simply Veterans Affairs. And then there's the Teamsters Union. And Mocks Crest, St. Johns, and Grants Pass. And how about Devil's Island, Devils Tower, and Devil Mountain? As the prophet Ezra so nicely put it, "And when I heard this thing, I rent my garment and my mantle, and plucked off the hair of my head and of my beard, and sat down astonied." A reasoned response.

A Special Possessive

We turn our attention now to the matter of the possessive before a gerund. Not infrequently Miss Grammar sees this overlooked and thinks people are simply not recognizing gerunds when they see them. Miss Grammar prefers to believe it is not a sign of moral decadence.

A gerund is an "ing" form of a verb used as a noun; the noun or pronoun modifying it should be in the possessive form.

> "I am concerned about your taking the job."
>
> "Was there any record of the client's writing to the plaintiff?"

A gerund is not to be confused with a participle—also an "ing" form of a verb but one that functions as part of a verb phrase (was laughing, had been finishing), as an adjective (the laughing children), or as a nonfinite verb: "The children, laughing hysterically, left the room."

> "The man sitting at the desk solved our problem."
> [This is a participle; "who is sitting" is understood.]
>
> "I don't like the girl reading."
> [This is a participle; "who is reading" is understood.]
>
> "I don't like the girl's reading."
> [This is a gerund; I like *her*—I just don't like the way she reads.]

The rule holds even when other words intervene:

> "With the exception of Mr. Green's occasionally parking in the area east of the access, all the actions have been accounted for."

Sometimes it is helpful to substitute the word *his* for the noun to see whether it sounds more natural than *he* or *him*. If *his* sounds better than the others, you are surely dealing with a gerund.

Double Possessive

Why do we say, "He is a friend of Bob's" instead of "a friend of Bob"?

We see an element of reciprocity at work: With "He is a friend of Bob's," we infer the likelihood that Bob likes him too. "He is a friend of Bob" would mean that he has Bob's best interests at heart but that Bob might not even be aware of that fact.

Where reciprocity is missing, so is the double possessive:

> "It could never be said that Fuller was a friend of the Church."
> "Jefferson was a friend of Democracy."

Miss Grammar also notices plurality at work: We say "the plays of Shakespeare" but "a play of Shakespeare's," suggesting that when one item from among many like items is singled out, the double possessive occurs. Thus, "we are friends of Bill's" implies that he has many such friends, and we are two of the many.

But the implication is not always plural. Consider:

> "Did you see that nose of his?"

What we see here is an idiomatic borrowing of the double possessive for emphasis; often the word *that* is included and there is a tone of annoyance, disbelief, chagrin, or amused derision.

> "She parked that car of hers right across the driveway."

Generally, we use the correct forms without thinking about them, no mean accomplishment when we see all the opportunities to go astray:

> "A friend of me, who always sticks that big nose of him in matters that are no concern of him, is waiting outside with a friend of us."

Inanimate Objects

Can an inanimate object take a possessive *s*?

Is there a:

> refrigerator's door
> car's window
> Oregon's statute of frauds
> opinion's holding
> statute's purpose
> complaint's prayer?

Madeline Semmelmeyer and Donald O. Bolander in *Instant English Handbook* 104 (1985) say, "Inanimate objects cannot possess anything," and that therefore it is better practice not to use the possessive forms for inanimate objects. But the authors are, in a sense, answering the wrong question. This is not a matter of possession at all, but of the attributive genitive case.

To illustrate: If I speak of *my* dentist or *my* hairstylist, I do not mean that I own these people, but rather that they are within the sphere of my experience—I take my business to them and rely on them.

The attributive genitive encompasses origin, possession, association with, adverbial expressions, characteristics, and measure, as well as a few other things. Not every apostrophe-*s* combination means possession. A glance at these expressions shows us how often we correctly write what looks like "possession":

> an hour's delay
> the earth's surface
> "Chief nourisher in life's feast" (Shakespeare)
> duty's call
> today's edition
> the water's edge
> New Year's Eve
> season's greetings
> a stone's throw
> a few minutes' quiet

There is no reason not to say "the statute's purpose," "the dog's tail" (some people insist that animals cannot "own" anything either), or "the book's cover." This is simply not a matter of possession; it just looks like it.

10

PROLIXITIES

Noun-Stacking

The long compound-noun phrase is to clarity and grace in a sentence as a flat tire is to speed and agility in a bicycle. With either one, as Bob Dylan used to say, "You ain't goin' nowhere." Wilson Follett called the noun-on-noun pattern "noun plague," *Modern American Usage* 229 (1966); Miss G. calls it noun-stacking. Here is an example:

> "With these principles in mind, we may now begin to formulate accident report information extraction rules."

That deadly thump, thump you hear is the flat tire—what on earth do those last five words (structurally all nouns) mean? To make a stab at determining the meaning, we must work backwards: "rules by which we extract information from reports of accidents."

Let's try another one:

> "The committee reports its suburban reconstruction evaluation studies need."

This must mean:

> "The committee reports that it needs to study evaluation of [or needs to study and evaluate?] reconstruction in the suburbs."

Miss G. hopes you now sense the real danger in writing these nouny sentences—it is not just that someone may not get your meaning; it is that your reader will impose his own translation on your work, perhaps to your sorrow.

Miss G. sees lots of noun-stacking in writing having to do with environmental law. This is typical:

> "These additional requirements lack soil sampling location specifics and minimum leak detection capacity statistics."

When Miss G. raises her genteel voice in protest, she is usually told that the Code or the Regulations or the Statute or the Experts or the Deity writes in Those Very Same Words. In that case, let's summon the sterling rule that unless something is quoted directly, we're not obliged to repeat an error.

Circumlocutions and Lawyerisms

Prolix, woolly	Simple, clean
abutting	next to
adequate number of	enough
adjacent to	next to
at the time when	when
be able to	can
be authorized	may
be unable to	cannot
contiguous to	next to
during such time as	while
excessive number of	too many
for the reason that	because
in the event that	if
or in the alternative	or

Prolix, woolly	Simple, clean
previous to	before
prior to	before
pursuant to	under, in accordance with
subsequent to	after
sufficient number of	enough
the reason being that	because
until such time as	until

Historically

"Historically, hazardous wastes were deposited into an on-site dry well."

It would be better to begin the sentence with *routinely* or *habitually* or *usually*—or with no adverb at all. *Historically*, so dear to the hearts of environmental lawyers, is better used to mean "having considerable importance or influence in history."

Overwriting

1. "The firm makes the maximum effort to utilize these two groups to the optimum possible extent."

Better: "The firm uses these groups as much as possible."

2. "RCA would have the ability to * * *."

Better: "RCA could * * *."

3. "This will occur in close temporal proximity."

Better: "This will occur at about the same time."

4. "The attorney just out of law school trying his first case often does not possess the inherently factual information necessary."

Better: "The inexperienced lawyer may not have all the facts."

RoboSpeech

"The visualization of the individual was made at 2 p.m."

Better: "I first saw him at 2 p.m."

An Odd Way to Put It

1. "The evidence was excessively speculative to support the award of damages."

Better: "The evidence was too speculative to support the award of damages."

2. "The normal time frame for a flooring inspection is once a month, and the normal time frame for CBA group meetings is on a weekly basis."

Better: "Flooring inspections are usually made once a month, and the CBA group usually meets once a week."

Prolix, Indeed . . .

"Vehicles must be secured when not in the immediate attendance of any individual. This means, if you cannot visually monitor vehicle access, it must be secured."
["Lock the van if you leave it unattended where you cannot see it."]

Miss Grammar wonders whether you can imagine your mother saying, "If I visually monitor you out in the street again, I'll skin you alive!"

SOME PRACTICAL MATTERS

Honorable and *Reverend*

Honorable is a title of respect given to judges and other high officials. It should not be used with surnames only. When it is used with a complete name, *the* is required; *the* is not capitalized unless it begins a sentence or is part of an address. Thus:

1. The Honorable Maria Stuart
   United States District Judge
   608 United States Courthouse
   620 S.W. Main Street
   Portland, Oregon 97215

2. Dear Judge Stuart:

3. When our client wrote to the Honorable Maria Stuart, he inadvertently perjured himself.

The title *Reverend* invites misuse, abuse, and generally illiterate treatment, probably under the influence of Western movies—a gunslinger who calls a friend "pardner" is probably going to call the preacher "Reverend" ("Padre," if the clergyman is a priest).

Reverend, as a title, is an adjective, not a noun; thus it is preceded by *the* (like *Honorable*):

1. The Reverend Joseph Morgan
    800 Monte Vista
    Salinas, California 93901

2. Dear Pastor Morgan:
    Dear Mr. Morgan:

3. Did you know that in April the Reverend Joseph Morgan will speak at the capitol?

4. I think it will be a privilege to hear the Reverend Mr. Morgan speak.

Absolutely unacceptable:

Have we paid the Reverend yet?

You must be tired, Reverend!

Tabulated Sentences

One of the best ways to avoid ambiguity is to set material out on the page in a form that makes clear how its parts relate to each other—the tabulated sentence. Miss G. recommends at least labeling parts of a long sentence with numbers if you don't want to go into tabulated structure.

Nontabulated

> If the company (1) defaults in paying rents, utilities, or license fees, (2) fails to provide proper maintenance of the grounds, (3) allows its tenants to waste forest resources, or (4) commits any public nuisance, the Lessor may enforce the security under the Lease.

Tabulated

> If the company
>
> (a) defaults in paying rents, utilities, or license fees,
>
> (b) fails to provide proper maintenance of the grounds,

(c) allows its tenants to waste forest resources, or

(d) commits any public nuisance,

the Lessor may enforce the security under the Lease.

It doesn't matter whether one uses numerals (1), (2), (3) or letters (a), (b), (c)—consistency within the document is a must, however.

Writing a tabulated sentence will also show you your own incoherence very quickly, if indeed you have erred:

If Lessor's premises are damaged,

(a) Lessee shall pay damages and a 10 percent surcharge; and

(b) if Lessor's premises are not damaged, Lessee's deposit will be returned to Lessee with 10 percent interest.

As we can see, this sentence falls apart—it makes no sense to say, "If Lessor's premises are damaged, Lessee's deposit will be returned," and it makes no sense to say, "If Lessor's premises are damaged, if Lessor's premises are not damaged." There is nothing like tabulated form to show up an incoherent statement.

Shortened Names of Entities

Names of parties, companies,[2] and other entities are frequently shortened or "defined" in legal documents. In what sometimes amounts to compulsive zeal, attorneys may overdefine, painstakingly (and painfully) shortening every label on the landscape. Such a practice invites ridicule, especially after six or seven names have been defined, names that could never be confused with any others anyway.

---

[2] *See* Bryan A. Garner, *A Dictionary of Modern Legal Usage* 128-29 (1987).

If Henderson Printing Company and Bemis Bag are simply referred to as Henderson and Bemis, no one will confuse one of these names with the other. It doesn't make things any more "legal" to use a parenthetical label; the shortened name may quietly be employed without fanfare.

Only when there is a real danger of mixing up similar names should we spell out parenthetically (and without *hereinafter*) what we're going to call them, as in this example:

> "Plaintiff William Haynes ('Haynes'), acting individually and not in his capacity as president of the Wm. S. Haynes Co. ('Company'), asks the court's approval of the following action."

The same holds true for individuals' names; there is neither sense nor safeguard in the slavish repetition of the surname, as in this example:

> "John Daggett ('Daggett'), Herbert Fried ('Fried'), Wiley Tweed ('Tweed'), and Stuart Little ('Little'), plaintiffs in the above-captioned matter, seek to have that judgment overturned."

These names should be given in full at the outset, then referred to consistently by surname without formal definition or labeling.

An appositive definition or label should match its antecedent; we should not write the following:

> "In the earlier litigation we objected to The Frederick Stone Company's ('Stone') motion for dismissal."

> *Better:* "In the earlier litigation we objected to the motion for dismissal made by The Frederick Stone Company ('Stone')."

Yeah and *Uh-oh*

From time to time secretaries, court reporters, and word processors are called on to transcribe informal expressions of assent, dissent, musing, or inquiry. In the interests of uniformity, Miss G. is providing a list of the preferred spellings of those expressions:

> yeah (not yea, yeh, or ya)
> uh-huh
> yep
> mm-hmm
> nope
> uh-oh
> unh-uh or huh-uh
> mmmm
> huh?
> uh
> (Eek! and Aargh! are seldom used)

et al. and *Esq.*

May we write a firm's name with *et al.* if the name won't fit on a label?

Miss Grammar thinks it unwise and unpolitic to dismiss important persons with an airy wave of the hand. It would be better to break the name into two lines or use a larger label: Friendly, Holt, Martin, Hale & Madden is a labelful, to be sure, but why risk what might be perceived as a snub of the last two or three?

In the United States, *Esq.* is used primarily by lawyers, and more often on the East Coast than on the West. Although it is thought that the title by derivation belongs only to males, it is common practice for women to use the title as well. As a matter of etiquette, one does not use it on oneself (as, for example, on a self-addressed envelope).

If anyone is bothered by appending *Esq.* to a woman's name, he or she may pretend that it stands for *esquiress*.

The Exclamation Point

Miss Grammar rarely addresses questions of punctuation because good style manuals and handbooks do an adequate job of providing information on the ins and outs of garden-variety punctuation. The exclamation point, however, wafts a spicy fragrance of its own and deserves special attention. Miss Grammar likes the terse advice of Jane Walpole, in *The Writer's Grammar Guide* 81 (1980): "Exclamation points hardly ever appear in factual writing, so forget about them." It must be pleasant to order people about. Miss Grammar thinks Jane should have ended her command with an exclamation point.

Actually, the mark appears all too often, in "factual writing" and elsewhere.

The exclamation point is customarily used:

1. After all exclamatory sentences, sentences that express surprise, emotion, or deep feeling:

"He wore brown shoes with a blue suit!"

2. After an interjection:

"Shoot! That was my best argument."

3. After commands:

"Send your order now! Don't delay!"

4. After an interrogative sentence that is intended to be exclamatory:

"How could the plaintiff say that!"

5. To add emphasis:

"Realize what this means!"

6. Within parentheses to serve as a knowing wink or dig in the ribs among friends:

"We won exclusive (!) film rights."

By this time, you may be thinking, "Oh! what nonsense! Lawyers never (!) use exclamation points! This has nothing to do with us!!"

Au contraire, dear readers—lawyers use exclamation points far more often than they should, to the detriment of their work and the amusement of their enemies. Sometimes it is hard to resist the temptation to kick a weak sentence in the hurdies, but appending an exclamation point to a mewling phrase is not the way to do it—at worst, you will end up sounding shrill and petulant; at best, your sentence will have gained an unfortunate gee-whiz flavor.

Miss Grammar has even seen *double* exclamation points in the work of harried, desperate attorneys trying to hammer home a point.

Consider the effect on the reader of all this figurative foot-stamping:

> "Assuming, without deciding (!), that the process of amelioration has been less than successful, defendants cannot suggest that they were denied due process. They admit they had access to all records before the hearing! They were clearly aware of the tolling of the statute!! Most important, they knowingly ignored every opportunity to present evidence on the jurisdiction issue!!! The trial court has correctly denied defendants' motion to set aside the judgment!"

If that isn't persuasive enough, consider the goofy, Valley-Girl quality imparted to stately English by the sprinkling of exclamation points:

> "Now Israel loved Joseph more than all his children, because he was the son of his old age! And he made him a coat of many colours! And when his brethren saw that their father loved him more than all his brethren, they hated him, and could not speak peaceably unto him! And Joseph dreamed a dream, and he told it his brethren: and they hated him yet the more!!"

Oh, wow!

Has Miss Grammar made her [exclamation] point or what!!?!

Fax

What is the correct usage for business and legal correspondence on business cards and letterhead, as well as in sentences? Do we use *telefacsimile, Telecopier, Telefax, facsimile,* or *fax*? Webster's Ninth New Collegiate Dictionary (1984) shows *telefacsimile* to be the correct word (but it is rarely used), *Telecopier* to be a trademark, *facsimile* to be for radio and wire transmissions (such as for overseas transmissions), and *fax* to be short for *facsimile*.

On business cards and letterhead it's wisest to list numbers like this, using the word *telecopy*:

TELEPHONE: (503) 555-3655
TELECOPY: (503) 555-3555

Some firms use: FAX: (503) 555-3555. That's fine, except that it perpetuates the notion that *fax* is an acronym. We need to stay away from *Telecopier*, to be sure, because it is a trademark.

As far as textual use goes, use *fax* for both verb and noun—no capital, no underscoring, no quotation marks, as in this example:

"After I fax the information to Harlan, I'll give you a copy as well as a copy of *his* fax if he faxes me an answer today."

In preparing bills, be careful that you do not write "review fax from Ms. Burton"; take the time to specify "review contract from Ms. Burton." We would not write "review Federal Express from Judge Roberts"; we would write "review agreement from Judge Roberts." How a document is sent or received is irrelevant.

Miss Grammar knows that *fax* seems a little bit unbuttoned, but dictionaries don't classify it as slangy, vulgar, colloquial, or even informal; it really is a respectable word.

High Noon

How are we to write *12 o'clock*? Is it *a.m.* or *p.m.*?

The period from midnight to noon is *a.m.*, meaning *ante meridiem*, "before noon." One minute before noon is 11:59 a.m. One minute after noon is 12:01 p.m. The clearest designation for 12 o'clock is to write or say *12 noon* or *12 midnight*.

We can say simply *noon* or *midnight* when we are speaking in approximate terms, but when we mean exactly 12, or when we are using other times expressed in figures, we should say *12 noon* or *12 midnight*.

The Virgule/Solidus

What does the diagonal line, usually called a slash, really mean? For example, in a trust deed reading "John Jones/Mary Smith as beneficiary," does that mean that *either* Jones or Smith is the beneficiary or that *both* are the beneficiaries?

In contending with the *virgule* (the formal name of the slash),[3] Miss Grammar is reminded of a line from Lewis Carroll's "Jabberwocky":

> "Beware the Jubjub bird, and shun
> The frumious Bandersnatch!"

In our case, we would do well to shun the frumious virgule, as will soon become apparent.

First, the virgule does have some more or less legitimate and useful employment:

1. to divide dates (8/3/88);

2. to divide fractions (3/4), although sometimes called a *solidus* when used to separate numerals;

3. to show line division in poetry (Sweetest love I do not go/For weariness of thee);

4. to indicate choice, as in a test (is/is not) or invitation (will/will not) or the debatable *and / or*;

5. to indicate *per* (miles/hour);

6. to show connection of some sort (Report filed by Donald Hastings/Los Angeles); and

7. to indicate that a person or thing has two functions (the owner/manager).

Notice that items 4 and 7 present the very problems that began this discussion: No. 4 indicates *or*, and No. 7 indicates *and*. How are we to know which is meant? It is better, Miss Grammar opines, *in the writing* to use a virgule only for *or* and to clearly state *and* when that is what is meant. In No. 7, the writer should say "the owner and manager."

---

[3] This mark is also called the diagonal, separatrix, shilling mark, slant, and stroke.

Most dictionaries will stress the "eitherness" of the virgule, and William Safire, in *I Stand Corrected* 404 (1984), draws our attention to the court's seeing it that way too, in *Miron Rapid Mix Concrete v. Bank Hapoalim*, 432 NYS2d 776, 777-78 (Sup Ct 1980). A check payable to "Revel/Miron Ready Mix" was endorsed and cashed by Revel *only*. Were both signatures necessary to properly negotiate the check? The court held that the check was properly paid with endorsement of only one of the named payees.

We see that a virgule can be of much more detriment than benefit, and you may be as puzzled as Miss Grammar as to why one would make out a check or trust deed to two persons, separating their names with a virgule. *And* or *or* would have been much the wiser choice.

And/Or

Miss Grammar is not fond of the *and/or* combination and knows she has lots of company. Either *and* or *or* is usually adequate, or another phrasing will do as well.

> 1. "All dwellings and/or other structures on the property are included in the contract."
>
> 2. "All dwellings and other structures on the property are included in the contract."
>
> 3. "All structures on the property are included in the contract."

If the writer wishes to keep the *and/or* distinction, he or she may easily do so with the phrase *or both*.

> 1. "Lessee will provide insurance covering fire and/or wind damages."
>
> 2. "Lessee will provide insurance covering fire or wind damages or both."

Even better:

> 3. "Lessee will provide insurance covering damages by
> fire or wind or both."

Comparatively Speaking . . .

Related to the *and* / *or* problem is the matter of a certain kind
of comparison. Phrasing a comparative construction can be vex-
ing indeed. Usually the frustrated author degenerates into a
state of fussing with *and* and *or*. Examples:

> 1. "Please deposit with American Express the greater of
> 30 percent of the March 1987 profits and $500,000."
>
> 2. "Please deposit with American Express the greater of
> 30 percent of the March 1987 profits or $500,000."

Better than 1 or 2 is:

> 3. "Please deposit with American Express either
> 30 percent of the March 1987 profits or $500,000,
> whichever is greater."

Note: If the options number more than two, use *greatest* or
least rather than *greater* or *lesser*.

Example:

> "Henderson is contractually bound to produce the
> proceeds of the stock sale, the income from Sage Ranch,
> or his life savings, whichever is least."

Judge Solomon (now deceased) said many years ago: "The
legal draftsman must write for unidentified foe as well as known
friend. He must write so that not only a person reading in good
faith can understand but a person reading in bad faith cannot
misunderstand."

An *A* or an *An*?

Why do we feed *a* dog but hunt *an* elephant? To facilitate pronunciation, as any child knows.

A word beginning with the *sound* of a vowel (not necessarily a vowel) is preceded by *an*—an aspersion, an envelope, an X ray.

A word beginning with the *sound* of a consonant (not necessarily a consonant) takes *a*—a book, a eulogy.

So far, so good.

A word beginning with an aspirated *h* takes either *a* or *an* depending on the speaker, the accented syllable, and the regional custom. Many people are likely to use *an* if a syllable other than the first is accented: an hysterical person, an historic occasion, but a huckleberry pie. Keep in mind that *a* is equally acceptable in all three cases here, but not when the *h* is silent, as in an honest mistake.

Now to the real problem: How do we choose between *a* and *an* when we are dealing with initials that may or may not form an acronym, like FSLIC?

If we know that everyone hears the letters as Fizzlick, we choose *a*: a Fizzlick document. But if most people spell out the letters as eff-ess-ell-eye-see, it would be *an* FSLIC document.

In preparing printed work, therefore, be sure to consider the *sound* of a word or set of letters as well as the looks: a NATO project, a UFO sighting, an FBI case.

12

SUBJECTS AND VERBS

None/Any

People regularly ask Miss Grammar whether *none* and *any* take singular or plural verbs. Fifty years ago, the answer—short and sweet—would have been *singular*. Now, matters are not so simple. Let us consider the various authorities; first the two unabridged dictionaries with their usage notes:

Random House:

> "Since NONE has the meanings 'not one' and 'not any,' some insist that it always be treated as a singular and be followed by a singular verb: *The rescue party searched for survivors, but none was found.* However, NONE has been used with both singular and plural verbs since the 9th century. When the sense is 'not any persons or things' (as in the example above), the plural is more common: . . . *none were found.* Only when NONE is clearly intended to mean 'not one' or 'not any' is it followed by a singular verb: *Of all my articles, none has received more acclaim than my latest one.*"

American Heritage:

> "*None* (pronoun) may take a singular verb or a plural one, according to 68 per cent of the Usage Panel. They specify a singular verb when *none* can logically be construed as singular (when *not one* or *no one* can be substituted for *none*): *None of us is wholly blameless.* A singular verb should also be used when *none* precedes a singular noun: *None of the laundry was really clean.* A plural verb should be used when *none* applies to more than one (when *no persons, not any of a group of persons or things* can be substituted for *none*): *None are more wretched than victims of natural disasters.* When *none* can be logically construed as either singular or plural, either a singular or plural verb is possible: *None of these books is (or are) really helpful.* In every case the verb and related personal pronouns and pronominal adjectives must agree in number: *none has his* (or *none have theirs*). According to 28 per cent of the Panel, *none* must always take a singular verb."

> "*Any* (pronoun) can take either a singular or plural verb, depending on how it is construed: *Any of these books is suitable* (that is, *any one*). *But are any* (that is, *some*) *of them available?*"

Following is what two handbooks on grammar propound.

John C. Hodges & Mary E. Whitten, *Harbrace College Handbook* 71 (10th ed 1986):

> "Subjects such as *all, any, half, most, none,* and *some* may take a singular or a plural verb; the context generally determines the choice of the verb form."

Morton S. Freeman, *The Grammatical Lawyer* 2 (1979):

> "By convention, *none* takes either a singular or plural verb, depending on the thrust of the thought to be conveyed. * * * When uncertain whether to use a singular or a plural verb, and if a decision must be made promptly, it is safer to choose the singular."

In other words, unless the context screams for the singular, you are well within grammatical bounds in using the plural.

Needs singular:

"None of the flour was usable."

Needs plural:

"We requested all the financial records of Bradley Corp. as well as personal ledgers and records of all officers, but none were provided."

Takes either:

"None of these suggestions (is)(are) worthwhile."

This has not been an easy transition for Miss Grammar, who was trained long ago to disregard the intervening prepositional phrase and go right for the verb—now the intervening phrase is said to control. But as Miss G. is fond of saying, in things grammatical, nothing is as permanent as change.

Shall, Will, and *May*

Shall and *will* in standard American usage have undergone substantial changes; Miss Grammar does not want to confuse things further by providing a history of those changes—it is enough to say that commonly we now use *will* for simple future declaration ("I will bring the books with me") and *shall* to mean "do you want me to?" ("shall I bring the books with me?").

In legal matters, things are different: *Shall* expresses orders. *May* expresses discretionary authority. *Will* expresses agreement.

A common error is known as the "false imperative." It is a false imperative to say, "The rent shall be due on the first day of each month"; the rent *is* due on that day. It is a false imperative to say, " 'Stockholder' shall mean any person who owns at least five shares * * *"; "Stockholder" *means* that.

You Say You Don't Get Tense?

Sooner or later, almost every attorney will pause in the middle of dictating or drafting, buffaloed momentarily by verb tense: past or present? The case being cited is definitely *past*, but the determinations made at that time still hold true today. What to do? Let's consider these examples:

> 1. "A similar distinction was recognized by the court in *Owen v. Jones*, 46 Or App at 105. The defendant tenant in that case sought abatement of its landlord's forcible entry and detainer action seeking possession of the rented premises. The plaintiff landlord had earlier instituted an action to recover damages against the tenant for failure to pay rent. The court held that because the primary relief in the forcible entry and detainer action is a judgment for restitution of the premises, it is significantly different from an action seeking a money judgment for an unpaid rent."

> 2. "*Rennie* supports our position because the court in *Rennie* recognized that where one of the claims fell within the exclusive jurisdiction of a tribunal that is incompetent to adjudicate the other claims, abatement is not available."

Now, are you absolutely positive of the tense, past or present, of the verbs in those examples? Probably not. How can we *know*?

The problem is not a basic knowledge of tense, which most of us possess—the concern is that tenses be kept in the proper sequence.

The tense of the initial verb tells us when the main action takes place, and all the other verb tenses in the paragraph express time in relation to that main verb. If the action in a subordinate clause takes place at the same time as the main action, then the verb must be in the same tense as the main verb (present with present, past with past, and so on).

If, however, the subordinate action took place before the main action, the subordinate verb must be in a past tense. Even though the two verbs are in different tenses, there is unity of tense. The tenses correctly express the sequence of happenings.

Past/Past

> "When the judge returned to the bench, the defendant made a rude noise."

Present/Present

> "As attorneys spend time with their clients, billable hours increase markedly."

Present/Past

> "Herb understands that the partnership has promised him a place."

Past/Prior Past

> "Herb learned that the partners had made promises to Jones a week earlier."

In English there is also a *general* rule of sequence that when a past indicative precedes (fear not, little flock; it will be made clear by example), a past-tense form must usually follow: "The firm wants to be ready when the new partner arrives," but: "The firm *wanted* to be ready before the new partner *arrived*."

> "The Oregonian said he was a young black scholar." [Even though he still *is* young, black, and scholarly.]

This sequence is not observed if something is represented as habitual, customary, characteristic, or universally true:

"He asked the clerk what time the office usually opens
[or *opened*]."

"He didn't seem to know that attorneys work late."

"The judge reminded them that honesty has always been
the best policy."

The present tense is often used to represent a state or activity
as still continuing:

"My partner told me this morning that the committee is
still at work on his proposal."

The present or future may slip in after a past indicative when
the reference is to a time still vividly felt as future at the time of
speaking:

"She told me this morning that she is going [or *will go*]
with us tomorrow."

Sometimes, incidentally, the literary present finds its way
into legal documents: "Judge Solomon reminds us in his treatise
to avoid cliches like the plague." Things in print seem to have a
kind of immortality, a persistent present—we quite comfortably
say, "As *A Tale of Two Cities* opens, Sidney Carton *waits* in the
wings."

And now what about the opening examples?

In 1 and 2, above, these changes should be made:

1. "detainer action *was* a judgment * * * it *was*
significantly different."

2. "that *was* incompetent * * * abatement *was* not
available."

Or: "where one of the claims *falls* within" [and the other
verbs remain in the present].

Not easy and not simple, this business of unity of tense, as
Miss G. is sure you'll readily agree. But into each life some

optative subjunctives and predicate appositives must fall, as grammarians like to put it.

A Time to Be Passive

Miss Grammar has railed frequently at the misuse of the passive voice, but she finds herself of a mind now to tell the whole truth—sometimes the passive is not only permitted, but even preferred.

First a brief reminder of what passive is:

1. Bob washed the car.   [*Active voice*]
2. The car was washed by Bob.
Or: The car was washed.   [*Passive voice*]

In the first sentence the verb is in the active voice because the subject is the *doer*—the subject is doing the washing.

The second sentence is written in the reverse order. The subject is now the *receiver* of the action. The doer may still be in the sentence as an agent, or he may have disappeared.

The passive is not always a poor choice. Sometimes the focus of thought or tact makes it preferable to the active voice, but conversely, sometimes responsibility can be evaded or a guilty person shielded. Observe:

Focus of Thought

"Our car was stolen yesterday." The car is what we are concerned about; we do not know who stole it.

"Almost all home mortgage loans nowadays are made for 25 to 30 years." Again, the agents are nebulous and go unnamed; it is the mortgage we are thinking about.

Tact

"Because the payment was not made on time, a small service charge has been added." [This is less likely to wound the reader than "Because you did not make the payment * * *."]

Evasion of Responsibility

"Your figures have been analyzed and found to be in error. The results of a new computation will be announced when the situation is judged appropriate." [Miss Grammar does not recommend that sort of weaseling.]

Shield for the Guilty

"Plaintiff's shoulder was also dislocated at the time of the accident." [By plaintiff's wife, who had swung a baseball bat at plaintiff's head and missed.]

Real trouble comes with the clumsy misuse or regular overuse of the passive:

> "His first speech was to be made by him in Salem."
> "The brief must be written by him tomorrow."
> "A chance will have to be taken."
> "The articles of incorporation shall be filed in the office of the secretary of state."
> [Who is in trouble if the filing is not done?]

The impersonal passive—it is felt, it is thought, it is believed—is thought elegant by some letter writers, but Fowler calls it "a pusillanimous shrinking from responsibility *(It is felt that your complaint arises from a misunderstanding. / It is thought that ample provision has been made against this contingency).* The person addressed has a right to know who it is that entertains a feeling he may not share or a thought he may consider mistaken, and is justly resentful of the suggestion that it exists in the void." H. W. Fowler, *A Dictionary of Modern English Usage* 439-40 (2d ed 1965).

Perhaps the best advice Miss Grammar can give on the passive is this: Know the difference between active and passive and be able to write either one. Choose the one that best suits your purpose of the moment and harmonizes with the style of the rest of your piece of writing.

We Is Enclosing . . .

Miss Grammar is often asked which verb is correct in this construction:

"Enclosed [is] [are] a copy of the complaint and a copy of the check."

"Enclosed [is] [are] a booklet and contract."

"Enclosed [is] [are] the name and address of the attorney."

"Enclosed [is] [are] the name, address, and telephone number of the arbitrator."

Miss Grammar is not going to supply the answers because she wants people to stop using this passive-voice pattern altogether—even when the verb is correct, it will not sound good, and someone somewhere will question it. Better to avoid the whole problem by casting the sentence in active voice:

"I have enclosed a copy of the complaint and a copy of the check." [or "*we* have enclosed"; "I am enclosing"; "I am sending you * * *."]

By making the enclosures the direct object of the verb in an active-voice construction, we don't even have to question which verb to use. Recasting is a wonderful editing tool and not used nearly often enough.

In the passage that follows, the vigorous, lean style of the paragraph is hamstrung by the passive voice in the last sentence:

> "We found that the Department of Energy did not obtain information about energy resources that federal offices were allocating to the state. The department needs this information so that it can determine how to redirect these resources when weather conditions change. It is thought that a system must be established by the secretary of the department so that information on weather conditions and fuel consumption may be gathered on a regular basis."

Those last four words provide Miss Grammar's parting shot. Let us eschew use of the tedious expressions "on a regular basis," "on a daily basis," "on an annual basis," and "on a frequent basis" and use "regularly," "daily," "annually," and "frequently" instead. The former style is akin to that of the weather forecaster who speaks knowledgeably of "shower activity" and "thunderstorm activity" instead of showers and thunderstorms.

The Demon Number

It's easy enough to say that subject and predicate must agree in number; particular applications, however, can generate confusion and awkward expressions. One source of difficulty is expressions that are plural in structure but singular in common usage or in the intent of the writer. Consider:

> "Ham and eggs [is] [are] my choice for breakfast."
>
> "Peanut butter and jelly [is] [are] popular with kids."
>
> "The plaintiff's name and address [appears] [appear] in the second paragraph of the complaint."

"Preparation and more preparation [is] [are] the key to successful trial advocacy."

"My position and the position of my client [is] [are] that this matter should go to the jury."

"Not only the plaintiffs but also their attorney [is] [are] in the judge's chambers."

"Not only the attorney but also his clients [is] [are] in the judge's chambers."

"The team of Jones, Jones & Jones [is] [are] in court giving it [its] [their] best effort."

When a group of words forms a single meaning (brandy and soda; pain and suffering), a singular verb is natural. The structure is sometimes called Siamese twins. Those of you who know her will think Miss Grammar made all this up, but she did not. Her idols, H. W. Fowler and Bryan Garner, made it up. Synesis is a grammatical principle governing subject-verb agreement whereby sense and logic take over. For example, *a handful* is singular ("A handful of clay is enough"), but in another context, its meaning is plural, and so is its verb ("Only a handful of young lawyers have any feeling at all for pro bono work"). The same goes for nouns of multitude (also called "collective nouns"): *team, family, jury, crowd, majority*, etc. They are treated as plural or singular at the writer's discretion. In Great Britain, we are likely to see "The family are expected at 3 p.m.," "The team are quite thrilled," and "The jury are filing in." Usually in this country, either we employ the singular in such an instance or we recast the sentence into a more comfortable form:

1. British: "The committee are not in agreement on the action they should take."

2. American: "The committee is not in agreement on the action it should take."

3. Recast: "The members of the committee are not in agreement on the action they should take."

Now to the opening examples: "Both ham and eggs *are* high in cholesterol," but "ham and eggs *is* a real power breakfast."

Similarly: "Peanut butter and jelly *are* not junk foods, although jelly may be classed by some nutritionists as 'empty calories.'" But: "Peanut butter and jelly *is* the best sandwich filling if you're in a hurry."

The determinant in each case is whether we think of the compound as a unit or not. The complement gives a valuable clue, but we must remember that in most cases, the verb follows the number of the *subject*, not of the complement: "The first crop *was* apples," not "*were* apples." But: "Apples *were* the first crop."

> "The best lunch you can eat *is* tacos," or "Tacos *are* the best lunch you can eat."

> "The plaintiff's name and address *appears* on the last page."
> [Seen as a unit.]

> "Preparation and more preparation is the key."
> [Siamese twins—words linked in pairs, used to convey a single meaning.]

> "My position and the position of my client *is* that this matter should go to the jury."
> [One position, shared by both parties. Contrast with "My position and the position of my client *are* miles apart."]

> "Not only the plaintiffs but also their attorney *is* in the judge's chambers." And: "Not only the attorney but also his clients *are* in the judge's chambers."
> [Whoever is nearer the verb controls the verb—also true in "either/or" and "neither/nor" constructions, as well as with plain "or." Even though logic may dictate that the plaintiffs and their attorney constitute a plural, grammar wins out. Remember that only *and* creates a plural, not *as well as*, *along with*, *together with*, etc.]

"The team of Jones, Jones & Jones is in court giving it their best effort" is indeed a sentence with a bothersome mixture of singular and plural. "The attorneys of Jones, Jones & Jones *are* * * * giving it *their* best effort" would be better.

Dummy Subjects (expletives)

An expletive (not the kind to be deleted) is a word, usually *it* or *there*, filling the position of another word so that the true subject can be postponed to follow the verb:

"There are two ways to do that."

Such a sentence is much easier for us to formulate than "Two ways to do that are there [exist]."

Sometimes a perfectly correct sentence, "That the negotiations broke down was unfortunate," can be improved and made to sound more natural in expletive form: "It was unfortunate that the negotiations broke down."

Expletives are often overused, but the grammatical construction itself is not necessarily weak or to be avoided. Writers should run both versions of their sentences through their minds and then make intelligent choices.

When multiple nouns follow the dummy subject, a problem in choosing the verb may arise. In "There are two ledgers, a catalog, and a diary on the desk," *are* naturally follows *there*. If we reverse the order of the items, though, putting the two ledgers last, we must choose between "There are a diary, a catalog, and two ledgers" and "There is a diary, a catalog, and two ledgers." The latter is more common because the singular noun is closer to the verb.

Sandwiched Verbs

A true economy of language—that is, the concise stating of ideas in the best possible way, using the fewest possible words—is a quality to be admired and emulated. A false economy—the cramming of verbs upon an overworked auxiliary or the pinchpenny reluctance to repeat an indirect object—is to be identified and shunned.

Sometimes we can successfully sandwich our verbs:

> "Allied can and should object to this motion."

But all too often, in an attempt at economy of language, we drift into murky waters. A verb acting in a dual role, especially with an auxiliary, may seem to function properly when it really does not:

> "Plaintiff can and has already taken this profitable step."

"Has taken" is fine, but we would never say "can taken." Although it might seem slow and wasteful, we must carefully say:

> "Plaintiff *can take* and has already taken this profitable step."

Consider this example:

> "There never has, nor will there ever be, another such opportunity to defend this much-maligned statesman."

Again, there is nothing for *has* to hang onto. We must write:

> "There never has *been*, nor will there ever be, another * * *."

Beware of leaving out a past participle and creating a non-parallel structure, as in:

> "I am concerned that your decision to voice these complaints at the staff meeting has or may damage the morale of the office."

We cannot say "has damage," but must take the time to write "has damaged or may damage."

13

PLAIN ENGLISH

Anyone would think that Miss Grammar enthusiastically embraces something with a name like "Plain English," but such is not the case. Oh, she embraces, all right, but only halfheartedly.

Draw your chairs closer, children, and let her tell you why.

What lawyers call the Plain English movement grew out of public frustration and general unhappiness with "legalese"—pompous, turgid, impenetrable prose. Lawyers readily admit its prevalence: Richard C. Wydick says, "We lawyers cannot write plain English. We use eight words to say what could be said in two." *Plain English for Lawyers* 3 (2d ed 1985).

Initially, in the late 1970s, Plain English was thought to be a remedy for consumer contracts—the average person was having a difficult time understanding a rental agreement or a time-payment plan for a refrigerator. The purpose of early legislation was " 'to enable the average consumer, who makes a reasonable effort under the circumstances, to read and understand the terms of so-called form contracts and the like without having to obtain the assistance of a professional.' " Unenacted Maine bill, *quoted in* David Mellinkoff, *Legal Writing: Sense and Nonsense* 211 (1982).

From the beginning, Plain English has been plagued by its own subjectivity, hoist with its own petard, so to speak. New York's legislation, for example, says that contracts must be written "in a clear and coherent manner using words with common and everyday meanings." That sounds a little like a semi-Biblical exhortation to "go and write well!"

Other laws, at the opposite end of the scale, present detailed tests by which to determine the readability of a document; the best-known tests are the Flesch test and the Gunning Fog Index. Miss Grammar will not weary you with the gruesome details, but she cannot resist the temptation to print this sentence, which scores *well* with the Flesch test:

> "The boy who the girl who hit the man in the white car kissed lives next door to me."

Contrariwise, this sentence is considered *less* readable because it has more two-syllable words:

> "This morning I got up and brushed my teeth and got dressed and ate breakfast and went to work." *Let the Rewriter Beware* 4 (1979) (Document Design Center pamphlet).

Plain English has also drawn criticism because of its "personalization"; i.e., using *I* and *you* instead of *lessor*, *mortgagor*, etc. The practice can ultimately *add* confusion of identity.

Miss Grammar's main quarrel with the Plain English movement is the assumption that simplifying the language will simplify the transaction; we know that is not so. It is not enough to say, "I agree to rent a car from you for $90 a month." The English is plain, but the true transaction remains complex and unaccounted for.

Our dealings are frequently complex, and the language that describes, provides for, and limits them may need to be complex too.

To Miss Grammar, Plain English means:

1. Using the active voice.

2. Using regular pronouns and articles, not *said* or *same*.

3. Avoiding unnecessary and difficult words.

4. Avoiding stuffing excess information into a sentence.

5. Avoiding nouns created from verbs and verbs created from nouns.

6. Keeping equivalent items parallel.

7. Unpacking stacked nouns (e.g., "suburban reconstruction evaluation studies need").

8. Avoiding multiple negatives (e.g., "not unlike an indifferent nonparticipant").

9. Deleting needless synonyms.

10. Avoiding legalese, computerese, and academese.

If we do these things, we will have done well indeed.

14

THE VERBING OF NOUNS

A very senior partner asked Miss Grammar point-blank: "Is *access* a good verb?" He had spotted this sentence: "The public can now access the river directly."

Miss Grammar's answer was, "Not really." No more than these nouns forced into verbhood:

> "Mr. Jones will office in the west wing."
>
> "I will copy Mr. Fleet with this letter."
>
> "I will carbon Mr. Fleet * * *."

We (and Miss Grammar uses that pronoun loosely) have fallen into TechSpeak or RoboSpeech, as one result of our computer age—and nouns used as verbs are not the only things that are giving grammarians fits. Odd terms now creep into everyday speech:

> 1. An NYPD narcotics officer, after cutting through steel rods to reach a cache of cocaine: "Well, just gettin' it in there musta been labor intensive."
> [must have been hard work]

2. "It would be more cost-effective to buy the giant size."
[economical, thrifty]

3. "These cocker pups are downright user-friendly!"
[gregarious, gentle, affable]

Miss Grammar hopes she is not alone in her wish to keep English a language of, for, and by human beings, not machines.

Miss G. has seen some other odd uses of language, specifically in the recounting of actions involving writs.

Witness:

1. "Judge Farnum praeciped the defendant to restore possession of the skating rink."

Better: "Judge Farnum issued a praecipe quod reddat, redirecting the defendant to restore * * *."

[Note: Although one often sees *praecipe* used as a verb, reliable dictionaries do not support such usage.]

2. "Anderson was habeas corpused to stand trial in Washington County."

Better: "A writ of habeas corpus was issued to remove Anderson for trial in Washington County."

3. "The court replevined John's Furniture Co. in its long-standing effort to retrieve its goods."

Better: "The court issued a writ of replevin in favor of John's Furniture Co., thus enabling it to retrieve its goods."

Or: "With the assistance of the court, John's Furniture Co. replevied its goods."
[Note: *Replevin* is a noun; *replevy* is a verb.]

The problem is again the employment of nouns as verbs. Granted, it may be a bit more trouble to write correctly, but the result is worth the effort.

Consider what might happen to our language if we forced words to perform other than their usual functions:

> "Arising early, Harold razored, toothpasted, suited, and cerealed. Then he sidewalked to the garage, Toyotaed downtown, and elevatored to the 33rd floor where he officed."

A well-meaning social worker was heard to remark, "Young women have trouble understanding cause and effect—that's why they're unable to contracept." Take it from Miss Grammar: there is no such verb as "to contracept."

Not quite the same, but just as disconcerting, are hyphenated verbs:

> "Senator Maureen Jones will be in the banquet room at 7:30 to answer questions and to idea-share."
> [Perhaps Senator Jones will have a spare moment to coffee-drink, people-meet, and baby-kiss.]

The Honorable George Joseph once brought this egregious verbing of nouns to Miss G.'s attention:

> "A judge shall not use * * * the power of the judge's office to disadvantage a lawyer unwilling to support the judge * * * or advantage a lawyer willing to support the judge * * *." Judicial Administration Committee Recommendation, OSB Annual Reports, 21.

Evidently there isn't a noun that can't be verbed.

Other nouns made into verbs:

> "A lot of our franchises are menuing helically shaped french fries. We have no idea what the competition is menuing."

> "We must set aside sufficient time to obsolete the manuals."
> [Is this a little bit like a teenager's over-the-hilling his parents?]

English is full of nouns that do double duty as verbs (*ship, list, process, paint, package,* etc.), but this latest crop of hybrids seems artificially cultivated.

15

WORDS

The D-Words

Discrete; Discreet

Discrete means "separate, individual, distinct"; *discreet* means "having or showing a judicious reserve in one's speech or behavior; respectful of propriety." To someone unfamiliar with *discrete*, the word might look like a typographical error, and the temptation to fix it might be too great to resist.

Gases are made of *discrete* units; and people who live in glass houses should be *discreet* and dress in the basement.

Disburse; Disperse

Disburse means to pay out. (Think of the university's *bursar* or your very own *bursae* in your knees, shoulders, etc., where you get *bursitis*. *Bursa* means "purse," and it indicates the little purselike places between joints * * *. Miss G. hopes she hasn't digressed to the point of no return; just remember that *disburse* refers to money.)

74

Disperse means to scatter in various directions, to distribute widely. Seeds can be dispersed, as can crowds. Pigment may be dispersed in oil, and Vitamin B is dispersed in rice polish to the extent that ten tons of polish yield only one ounce of vitamin.

Debut

Debut, a noun, meaning a first public appearance or the beginning of a career or course of action, is not established as a verb, despite its being recorded in the Oxford English Dictionary as having been in use in 1830. Nowadays we see *debut* as a verb used both transitively ("the company will debut its new roadster in 1994") and intransitively ("the dancers debut here next week"). Of course—and Miss G. loves to hammer this nail home—just because fashion favors this usage right now doesn't mean it's correct or attractive. Come to think of it, Miss G. feels the same way about spandex clothing.

Drug [Dragged]

Miss Grammar recently threw down a best-selling novel and danced upon it when she found *drug* used repeatedly instead of *dragged*. *Drug* belongs with *snuck* [sneaked], *throwed* [threw], and *flang* [flung]. For heaven's sake.

Dived, Dove, and Div

What is the past tense of *dive*? William Safire in *I Stand Corrected* 115 (1984) says, "*Dove* is * * * an aberration, almost a mistake, based on the past tense of *drive*." We say *drive, drove, driven*, but we may not say *dive, dove, diven*. Most usage notes permit *dove* in informal usage, but recommend *dived* in formal usage. Interestingly, Webster's Third New International unabridged lists *div* as a substandard alternative. That is a new one on Miss Grammar. She will stick with *dived* (and *lighted* instead of *lit*). When in doubt, choose the first form listed in the dictionary.

Dictionaries

Speaking of dictionaries, Robert C. Cumbow is pretty darned exercised about them in general:

> "Our lexicons have become like competing television news teams, trying to one-up one another. A usage—no matter how inappropriate, retrograde, or downright wrong—that gains a modicum of popular acceptance is now welcomed with open arms * * *. Dictionaries become destroyers * * * of the language when they rush to record an erroneous * * * usage merely because it has become popular. Dictionaries have become levelers of language, refusing to recognize that a majority often can be wrong." *The Subverting of the Goeduck*, 14 U Puget Sound L Rev 761 (1991).

Miss Grammar has deep thoughts about that—she thinks of dictionaries as *descriptive* rather than *prescriptive*. Dictionaries aren't really about "right and wrong" as much as they are about recording the ways people use words. The American Heritage Dictionary is especially valuable because of its usage notes, often mentioning along with a questionable form the percentage of its Usage Panel members who find the usage acceptable or not. The Usage Panel has about a hundred members—novelists, essayists, poets, journalists, writers on science and sports, public officials, and professors. *Debut* as a verb, for example, is disapproved of by 97 percent of the Usage Panel. Another example: *flammable* is as acceptable as *inflammable* in all areas of speech and writing to 61 percent of the Usage Panel. These kinds of figures allow one to know exactly how monstrous is the gaffe that one is about to make before one makes it. Or—how monstrous is the gaffe that one has *already made* and cannot possibly fix. Such a comfort.

Cause and Effect

Because, *since*, and *as* are not interchangeable.

Because is the most specific of the conjunctions used to express cause or reason and always indicates an unequivocal causal relationship: "I stayed behind because I was studying." (Miss Grammar discourages the use of *for* in place of *because*. *For* (after a comma) is less direct in indicating cause; the elements it links are more independent: "He resigned, for he found the workplace unpleasant." *For* is also the favorite conjunction of the writers of sentimental novels.)

Since is often a weak form of *because*, but its connotation of time implies that what it introduces makes the preceding matter follow by logical sequence or inference: "I have worried since I filed the brief."

As is the weakest in indicating cause and must be used with great care to avoid confusion with mere reference to time: "As the MARY DEANE was sinking, a tugboat approached." Note the ambiguity: Did the tug simply happen on the scene, or did it draw near to render aid?

Even if there is no question of ambiguity, the style or sound of *as* used in place of *because* is unpleasant and unprofessional; one's Aunt Tillie would use such language in her personal letters: "We are going to Cousin George's house this weekend, as we are celebrating his birthday."

Because—The Never-Ending Story

How can such a plain word cause so much fancy trouble?

> "They did not vote against the measure because they were trying to pacify the Committee."

Does this mean that their wish to please the Committee caused them to refrain from voting? Or does it mean that they *did* vote against the measure, but for a reason having little to do with the Committee?

When *because* follows a negative clause, does *because* disclaim a reason why a thing was done—or does it provide a reason why a thing was *not* done? Depending on the meaning intended, the above sentence would have worked better written like this:

> "Because they were trying to pacify the Committee, they did not vote against the measure."

or:

> "They voted against the measure but not because they were trying to pacify the Committee."

We cannot safely rely on an inserted comma to resolve the ambiguity; many writers use the comma idiosyncratically, and besides that, an excellent guideline in legal writing is that a sentence should be susceptible of one meaning only, even if punctuation is removed. David Mellinkoff says:

> "Sometimes punctuation is inadvertently omitted or misplaced in typing or typesetting. Sometimes it is overlooked by hasty readers. Try not to rely on punctuation alone to give meaning to what you are writing." *Legal Writing: Sense and Nonsense* 57 (1982).

Because can make a mess even when it does *not* follow a negative clause:

> "Finally, Swift is aware that the fraud case will be tried because it is already at issue."

Does this mean Swift's awareness is a result of the case's being at issue? Or does it mean that the fraud case will be tried because it is at issue?

In the same document, this appeared:

> "Father is in privity with daughter when father acts as administrator of his daughter's estate because he is in control of the action."

Is father in privity because he is in control? Or does father act as administrator because he is in control?

The fog lifts when we begin the sentence differently:

> "When father acts as administrator of his daughter's estate, father is in privity with daughter because he is in control of the action."

Because Revisited

Because can produce trouble all on its own, but when we encounter a double or even triple *because*, we really are in for it:

> "Employer's decision to terminate a Swedish inventory clerk was supported by business necessity because plaintiff did not adequately perform his job because of an inability to speak and understand English."

There are worse syntactical crimes than this, to be sure, but the sentence is nevertheless a bit unsettling.

> *Better:* "* * * did not adequately perform his job as a result of his inability to speak and understand English."

A *triple* use of *because* thuds against the reader's brain:

> "A member of the panel decided to speak out because the claimant had threatened the panel because the claimant feared being punished because he had given false testimony."

There are several ways to recast this sentence; Miss G. offers one:

> "Because the claimant (fearing punishment for his false testimony) had threatened the panel, a member of the panel decided to speak out."

Purposeful

> *Example*: "A lesser degree of purposeful abuse is necessary in an employer/employee relationship."

Purposeful means "having purpose, determined, resolute, full of meaning, significant." Here, *deliberate* would have been much better. Frequently, *on purpose* is what's needed.

Forward

Then there is the unfortunate *forwarded*.

> *Example*: "Howard wrote the letter and forwarded it to Felix the same day."

Here, *sent* is better. To forward means to send something on that we have received from someone else, often to a new address.

Visualize

Next we have *visualize*, which means "to recall or form mental images or pictures."

> *Bad*: "When the mortgage department visited the downtown area and actually visualized the finished building, all the members were impressed."
>
> *Worse*: "Orson Turner headed the investigative team and announced it to the group at large when he visualized the ledger."

In each case a simple *saw* or *could see* is better.

Now comes the much more amusing accidental misuse of a word, the true malapropism:

> "The van passed the care in an erotic manner."
>
> "Special today on harsh brown potatoes."
>
> "I highly recommend Janie for rolls in which speed, accuracy, and a good personality are required."

If I Were . . . If I Was . . .

The subjunctive mood is called for when we are dealing with a condition contrary to fact:

> "If I were rich [but I'm not], I would visit the lemurs in Madagascar."

When the *if* clause is only a condition, one not necessarily contrary to fact, we use the indicative (as opposed to the subjunctive), as in:

> "If I was absent, no doubt I had a good reason."

Or:

> "If the door was open longer than an hour, the new closet probably flooded."

We see clearly the uncertainty in these last two examples; it is only when we are *certain* that a condition is not so that we say "if it *were*":

> "If it were raining [but it's not], I'd try out my new umbrella."

If we can state the opposite (the contrary condition) clearly, we use the subjunctive:

> "If he had been in the office this morning [but he wasn't], I would have seen him."

But:

> "If he was in the office this morning [maybe he was], I did not see him."

> "If he left this job [he probably won't], he would take a teaching position."

But:

"If he leaves this job [maybe he will], he will take a teaching position."

Sometimes fiddling with the word *should* will help you determine whether you need subjunctive mood or indicative. In the following sentence, we could easily say, "Should Hayden Island be fenced off," and that tells us that we need subjunctive, i.e., *were*.

"Mr. Jones reported that if Hayden Island were fenced off and condemned, this would result in great financial loss."

Miss Grammar recommends your employment of *should* to determine mood but hopes you will eschew its actual use. Not only is it precious, it can also be misleading. When Miss Grammar recently heard a newscaster say, "Should your child eat the leaves of a plant or drink tea made from weeds," she uttered a horrified "Of course not!" only to hear the rest of the sentence—"call the poison clinic and save some of the plant."

If and *Whether*

What is the difference between *if* and *whether*?

Whether is used to introduce the first of a set of possibilities or alternatives. The second may be stated or merely implied.

"We need to know whether the station is open [or not]."

If means "in case that, granting that, supposing that, on condition that."

"Leave if you want to."
"I'll leave if you will."

Here is a common misuse of *if* when *whether* is needed:

"Martin did not know if the bank had already decided that point on Friday [or not]."

When there is a sense of the alternative, we use *whether*.

"I don't know whether [or not] I will ever see Portland again."

"I will take that trip up the Willamette if I ever see Portland again."
[*If* is required here because there is no sense of an alternative.]

When *whether* is discussed, people are sure to ask whether they must include *or not* or not. It would be wise to leave it out in that last sentence, for obvious reasons. But speaking generally, the writer's preference should prevail. We *must* include *or not*, however, when equal stress is given to the alternatives, as in:

"The hearing will be held whether or not the parents appear."

"The wedding will take place whether it rains or not."

Without the *or not*, this kind of sentence makes little sense:

"The wedding will take place whether it rains."

If the *or not* is just a filler, we may leave it out:

"I do not know whether the judge will speak to me [or not]."

First; Firstly

If a paragraph begins with the word *first*, must the following paragraphs use the introductory words *second* and *third*?

The Gregg Reference Manual 260 (7th ed 1992) says to "use the forms *first, second, third* (NOT firstly, secondly, thirdly)." Bryan Garner in *Modern Legal Usage* 218 (1987) says the same, although on page 243, surprisingly, he says, "Many stylists prefer using *first* over *firstly* even where the remaining signposts are *secondly* and *thirdly*."

Obviously, this screams for Miss Grammar's resolution: The terms should be parallel, either all with "ly" or all without, and because *first*, *second*, *third* seem to be preferred, Miss G. chooses those.

Quitclaim

Writers often ask how to spell *quitclaim*, as verb, noun, and adjective. Conflicting answers abound, from the statutes to Black's to CLE publications, but the newest dictionaries call for spelling *quitclaim* as one word in all its forms. Miss Grammar finds that tidy and pleasant. Like many compounds, *quitclaim* has evolved from its two-word form, through its hyphenated form, and now into its final one-word or "solid" form. The last stage is almost always final.

That

Disputes often arise concerning the use of *that*. For example:

> "Mother has remarried and asserts that her remarriage is a change of circumstances."

> "It should be noted that the hearing was held in March of 1988."

Some writers believe *that* is overused and unnecessary in the above sentences. Others think *that* is necessary to tie the sentences together.

That is a subordinating conjunction here, laboring to connect a noun clause to a main clause.

In the first sentence, *that* is preferred. One hears many reasons for the preference—among them the distinction between formal and informal writing—but the real reason is to prevent misreading. Whenever a noun or pronoun in the second part of the sentence can be taken for the direct object, we must use *that*. Observe:

> "Attorneys will argue the case taken as an example may impact land-use law as we know it."

Almost every reader will initially perceive the sentence as "Attorneys will argue the case."

In the example, less dramatically, "Mother asserts her remarriage."

The second sentence, without *that* ("It should be noted the hearing"), does not operate in exactly this way, but it still gives the reader pause—it reads almost like German syntax, something like, "It should be heard the music."

Sometimes, with verbs like *believe, suppose, think*, etc., we do very well to omit *that*:

> "I believe this is going to make a real difference."
> "He confessed he did not know the reason."

Many times *that* is overused and unnecessary. The trick is in knowing when it's needed. Miss Grammar recommends the direct-object test for many questionable cases.

Negative Thinking

A peculiar mistake crops up too frequently for it to be merely a typographical error; it is the misuse of a negative. Here are two examples:

> "There are not any indications of counsel's agreeing with us."
> "There are not substantial income tax savings."

In both of these sentences *no* is required as the modifier of the noun: no indications and no savings.

Except for certain abundant idiomatic expressions in informal speech ("not a thing"; "he hadn't any idea"), we use *no* before a noun or adjective-noun combination, when the idea expressed is that something does not exist, and *not* before a verb.

> "There was no hint of his cooperation."
> [But "That was not a hint—it was an order." We use *not a* to indicate that a given item is *not* one thing, which is evidently assumed, but rather another.]

Especially in the plural, as in the opening examples, we need *no*:

> "There are no books in the library on that subject."

No may be used with a comparative:

> "He is no better."

No may be used before an adjective to convey the opposite of the adjective's meaning:

> "His recovery was no small miracle."

No may be used before a noun to convey the opposite of the noun's meaning:

> "You're no Jack Kennedy."

No may mean "not any":

> "He had no money."

Miss Grammar wishes to emphasize that these guidelines are only for the most correct *formal* English; she is all for permitting the use of every barbarism one wishes on the back porch.

But . . .

A weed cropping up lately in Grammarland is the colloquial use of *but* when *only* is needed.

> "I had but one opportunity to reach him."
>
> "There was but one woman on the committee."

At one time *but* used as *only* was in relatively common use, but that is no longer the case. It is much wiser to use *but* as a preposition, with the meaning of "except" ("he does nothing but complain") and *only* when we mean "only."

Similarly, the colloquial *can't help but* should be replaced in written English with *cannot help*. ("He cannot help criticizing the management.")

Place

Not the same as *put*, which is usually the better choice. *Place* implies care and precision in bringing something to a certain position: "He placed the tripod six inches from the blossoms."

> "The clerk always places [read *puts*] the judge's chambers in order."
>
> "Defendant never had time to place [read *put*] his foot on the brake."
>
> "Claimant experiences severe pain when she places [read *puts*] her head down."

Individual

Not a substitute for *man, woman,* or *person*. *Individual* should be reserved for instances when one wishes to distinguish a single person from a group.

> "It was right at noon that the individual [read *man*] approached the judge's chambers with a handgun."

Purchase

No improvement over *buy*. But as a noun, *purchase* is useful indeed, both for "the thing you bought" and in this sense:

> "The frantic snake could find no purchase on the tiled floor."

Provided That If . . .

Most instances of *provided that* can be better written simply with *if* or *but*:

> "Chapter 11 of the Code allows for an orderly liquidation of assets of the debtor, provided that [read *if*] the debtor complies with the requirements of Chapter 11."

> "No claimant shall be allowed to reapply, provided that [read *, but*] if the Referee finds that the first application was inherently invalid, a claimant may submit a fresh application."

Ordinarily, *provided* means "as long as" or "if" or "except." Sometimes writers use it to mean "it is provided," in the sense that this is how things will be:

> "Provided further that borrowers may not elect any interest period ending later than the conversion date."

Such employment of *provided* creates a sentence fragment and should be stricken; the plain facts are enough: "Borrowers may not elect."

In this sentence, *provided that* is appropriate because another *if* is already present:

> "Secured claims may be restructured, provided that if such claims are restructured, they are paid within the term of the plan."

Hopefully

Grammarians have been crabbing about *hopefully* for years, among them Edwin Newman:

> "People say, 'Hopefully, something will happen.' They could, and they did for so long, use the simple and straightforward, 'I hope.' They don't say, 'Hopelessly, nothing will happen.'" *Strictly Speaking* 49 (1974).

There is no small controversy about this matter, and Miss Grammar should not have been surprised (but she was) to find that at least two dictionaries are in disagreement. First, the American Heritage (1992) usage note:

> "Writers who use *hopefully* as a sentence adverb, as in *Hopefully the measure will be adopted*, should be aware that the usage is unacceptable to many critics, including a large majority of the Usage Panel."

Now that is solid stuff. Less so the strange pronouncement from the Random House unabridged (1987) (usage note):

> "Although some strongly object to its use as a sentence modifier, HOPEFULLY meaning 'it is hoped (that)' has been in use since the 1930's and is fully standard in all varieties of speech and writing. Hopefully, tensions between the two nations will ease. This use of HOPEFULLY is parallel to that of certainly, curiously, frankly, regrettably, and other sentence modifiers."

Such logic. Many wrongheaded expressions have been in use since the 1930s, indeed since the days of Noah, and they have never become "fully standard." Miss Grammar is not, as some low-minded persons might suggest, picking on this opinion because it is at odds with her own; rather, she picks because its reasoning is faulty and its conclusion wrong. The use of *hopefully* is *not* parallel to that of the other modifiers. May we take them one by one:

1. "Certainly, the fiend will make another appearance." ["It is certain that * * *."]

2. "Curiously, the door to the dead man's chamber was locked from the inside."
["It is curious (odd) that," not "I am curious."]

3. "Frankly, my dear, I don't give a damn!"
[Merely an abbreviation of "Speaking frankly" or "Frankly speaking" followed closely by its referent, "I."]

4. "Regrettably, we shall have to ensure that you never work again."
["It is to be regretted that * * *" *or* "it is regrettable that * * *" *or* "we regret that * * *" *or* "one regrets that * * *."]

The pattern becomes clear. The true sentence modifier can be restated gracefully with an expletive, or dummy subject (it is certain, it is regrettable, it is curious), but *hopefully* cannot: "It is hopeful that" will not work, because only a person or an animal can be hopeful, not an inanimate set of circumstances. We can sensibly say only "*I* am hopeful that" or "the dog is waiting hopefully for his dinner."

This entire muddle has probably come about because English lacks an impersonal "ly" word meaning "it is to be hoped." Other languages are better equipped. German, for example, has *hoffnungsvoll* (hopeful, *adjective*) and *hoffentlich* (it is to be hoped; I hope, *adverb*).

The New York Times Manual of Style and Usage 95 (1976) winds it up for us:

> "*hopefully* means in a hopeful manner, and its use should be confined to that meaning: *They sought hopefully for the solution so desperately needed.* Do not use *hopefully* in this sense: *Hopefully, they will find the solution so desperately needed.* The intended meaning in such a case is *they hope to find, it is hoped* (parenthetical) or *it is hoped that* or some equivalent phrase, and one of them should be used. The foregoing, it is hoped, will clear up this troublesome matter and enable us to move on hopefully to solutions of other problems."

Miss G. hopes this discussion will help.

Forthcoming or Forthright?

A politician urges a foreign government "to be as forthcoming as possible"; a talk-show host comments that a guest has "certainly been entirely forthcoming" on the subject of his arrest for drug trafficking. Miss Grammar opines that *forthright* is the better choice in these instances.

Forthright means straightforward, frank, direct, and candid.

Forthcoming means approaching, about to appear, or available—sometimes simply coming forth. Properly used:

1. "The forthcoming election will decide everything."
2. "The money for the new building will not be forthcoming."
3. "The prince's forthcoming was the high point of the palace tour."

Upcoming, Advise, and Indicate

Miss Grammar finds herself frustrated by the ubiquitous misuse of these three words. In the interest of clarity and good style, she wishes to persuade her readers guilty of such misbehavior to mend their ways.

Upcoming

Increasingly used but still not as well established as synonyms like *forthcoming*, *coming*, and *approaching*. "The upcoming election" is acceptable to only 49 percent of the American Heritage Dictionary Usage Panel. "The *coming* election" is better.

Advise

Not to be substituted for *tell*, *inform*, or *notify*. *Advise* means to give advice to, to counsel: "Phillips should advise his client not to sign." Using *advise* in the sense of *notify* or *inform* is incorrect. For example, "Please advise me of your decision" should be changed to "Please *notify* me," and "My secretary just advised me it is raining" should be changed to "My secretary just *told* me."

Indicate

Not to be substituted for *say* or *write*. *Indicate* means primarily to demonstrate or point out, to serve as a sign, symptom, or token of: "The cracking of the ice indicates a change in temperature." Therefore, you will not want to write, "Roberts indicated in my office yesterday that he would like to retract his statement," unless the client was gagged and signaling with semaphores.

Infringe

Does one infringe *upon* or simply infringe?

Just plain *infringe* is a transitive verb (has a direct object) and means to commit a breach or infraction of something, to violate or transgress: thus, to infringe a copyright; to infringe a rule.

Infringe as an *in*transitive verb, and usually followed by *on* or *upon*, means to encroach upon or to trespass upon: "Don't infringe upon his privacy."

Generally, the very concrete item—an oath or an agreement, say—will call for the transitive verb, the first one above. The second, the intransitive, has a less strict interpretation.

Literally and Physically

Overheard: "My client was literally climbing the walls!" Not unless the client was Spiderman. *Literally* means "really, actually," as opposed to "figuratively." *Literally* is misused in many legal documents: "Johnson literally covered the ground in an attempt to find the missing strip-bolt."

Physically is also turning up unnecessarily and all too often: "Defendant Holt had physically placed the files in his safe." As opposed to *spiritually*? What is meant here? Perhaps that Holt placed the files there *himself.* Or placed them there *personally.* Or *actually* placed them there.

What about this: "Defendants conducted a physical inventory." We think the writer means that defendants looked at or touched the goods, rather than surveyed a balance sheet of some sort, but the usage is still inferior to this: "Defendants conducted a complete inventory" [or "on-site" or "on the spot"].

Which/That

Whether to use *that* or *which* to introduce relative clauses is troublesome; it is perhaps the most common little gaffe committed by writers today. It doesn't help, either, that the British are much less scrupulous than we are or that many otherwise sound handbooks have given up and decided that the two words are interchangeable. They are not. Once you really understand the difference, you will become somewhat sensitized to the improper usage, and you will see errors everywhere.

It may be helpful to have a little review of restrictive (essential) and nonrestrictive (nonessential) clauses.

A restrictive clause begins with *that*; it defines and limits its antecedent, and there is a sense of pointing or of identification:

> "A dog that bites is probably going to cost his owner a great deal of money."

Notice the absence of commas.

A nonrestrictive clause begins with *which*, preceded by a comma. It provides nonessential information:

> "A dog, which is often a fine substitute for a handgun, provides companionship as well as protection."

In this sentence, the information enclosed within the commas is a kind of "aside"—interesting information, but not *essential* to the main meaning: A dog provides companionship as well as protection.

For easy reference, you might consider memorizing these simple sentences:

> "This is the house that Jack built."
>
> "This house, which Jack built in 1910 for his mother, is in need of paint."

Miss Grammar fervently hopes you can see the wrongness of *which* in this sentence:

> "Each boy made a list of books which he read frequently."

Comprised/Composed Of

Comprised of does not legitimately exist; it is a bastardization affected by those for whom *composed of* is thought to be too plain.

> "By definition, the whole comprises the parts; the parts do not comprise the whole, *nor is the whole comprised of its parts*." American Heritage Dictionary 274 (1981) (emphasis added).

Thus: The Union comprises 50 states. Fifty states compose the Union.

We may not say, "The Union is comprised of 50 states."

Due To/Because Of

Due to is often used where it would be better to say *on account of*, *through*, *owing to*, and especially *because of*.

Miss Grammar hopes your ears are offended by "I am leaving due to the excessive noise," but not by "The collapse of the roof was due to the load of snow resting on it."

Due to is always acceptable as a predicate adjective following some form of the verb *to be*. After other verbs ("He hesitated due to fear") the phrase is not so apt. [Technically, and for those who care, we are questioning the use of *due to* to introduce an adverbial phrase that assigns the reason for, or cause of, the action denoted by a nonlinking verb.]

To be sure, the careless use of *due to* is employed widely in spoken English; some grammarians have thrown up their hands and given up, moaning about "offending usage among the illiterates," but Miss Grammar thinks it is at least worth the effort of presenting these simplified guidelines:

1. After *is, was, were, has been*, etc., use *due to*;

2. After other verbs, use *because of* or something else.

Commence or Begin?

At a writing seminar, Miss Grammar heard a possibly apocryphal story involving clients who, when told their new lease would commence in three days, packed up and prepared to move out. To them, *commence* meant the end of things, just as it had at high school commencement.

Since then, Miss G. has found herself ruminating upon every use of *commence* and wondering whether *begin* might be a better choice.

Rarely do we find words that truly mean "the same" as other words. Connotations abound and histories intrude. And so it is with *commence* and *begin*. Dictionaries, including the Oxford English Dictionary, declare that *commence* is just the same as *begin*, but when we turn the words over in our minds, we find subtle differences. Fowler's *Dictionary of Modern English Usage* 97 (2d ed 1965) states:

> "*Begin* or *start* is the word always thought and usually said, but it is translated sometimes before it is said, and often before it is written, into [*commence*] * * *."

Commence suggests to Miss Grammar a deliberate initiation of activity, perhaps following a period of sober reflection. Thus, we would *commence* a civil action but *start* a fight.

In describing very formal exercises or ceremonies (or legal actions) we would use *commence*, but *begin* is better for ordinary use. It sounds very stilted to say, "Jones commenced living in Pasadena." *Begin* is also preferred when introducing an infinitive: "In Oregon, the statute *begins* [not *commences*] to run on the date of the wrongful act."

Start suggests physical movement, usually abrupt—we start running or laughing or writing. We *begin* to believe it might be wise to *start* talking before litigation *commences*.

Lawyers use *commence* more than other people do. It isn't surprising to see the word drift into general use; neither is it desirable.

Less/Fewer

One hopes the confusion between *less* and *fewer* isn't *growing*. *Fewer* is used for things that can be counted and *less* is used for things that cannot: "There are fewer calories in this cake than one would think." "There is less nourishment in this cake than in that apple." Similarly, but speaking very generally, we should use *over* as a preposition ("She threw him over the wall") or adverb ("Turn the rocks over") and *more than* to mean "more than": "There were more than a dozen people there," *not* "There were over a dozen people there."

Use/Utilize

Lawyers overutilize the word *utilize*, evidently believing it sounds more significant than plain old *use*, just as some writers think *indicate* carries more weight than *say*.

As Miss G. is fond of remarking, there are few equivalents in language. *Utilize* is not an elegant variation of *use—utilize* means to make do with something not really intended for that purpose. You might *utilize* a fork to coax toast from a reluctant toaster, but that is not the purpose for which the fork was intended. We *utilize* a screwdriver to pry the lid from a can of paint, but we *use* the same screwdriver to tighten a screw on a cabinet.

Seen recently in a memorandum:

> "Counsel finished writing his report on the last day of September, utilizing a Bell helicopter."

Counsel might have done better with a pencil or a typewriter. Perhaps *utilizing is* appropriate here, when we consider the purposes for which a helicopter is intended, but the sentence is still a fine non sequitur.

Respectively

This overworked word appears frequently (and often unnecessarily) in legal writing. When needed, it is a useful tool, but when not, it is as pointless and distracting as mittens on a mackerel.

Because it intrudes so often, Miss G. suggests that otherwise astute adults may not have a clear idea of its function—to prevent misunderstanding in the pairing of one thing with another:

> "James, Carol, and Dennis spoke to the board, the committee, and the council, respectively."

Without *respectively*, we would think that each person mentioned spoke to all three audiences, when actually James spoke to only one (the board), Carol to only one (the committee), and Dennis to only one (the council).

When there are no clear sets of things to be matched, we do not need *respectively*; it becomes excess baggage and can even lead a careful or compulsive reader to abandon the thread of your story while he tries to match up the unmatchable:

> "They are residents of Oregon, Florida, and Nebraska, respectively."

Only if we have three names to put with the three states do we need *respectively*:

> "Hillman, Booker, and Rawlings are residents of Oregon, Florida, and Nebraska, respectively."

In case anyone is having trouble following this, we see that Hillman lives in Oregon, Booker in Florida, and Rawlings in Nebraska. Get it?

We should know, too, that *respectively* has no business doing duty as stand-in for *respectfully*. Miss G. has seen "respectively submitted" more often than she ever cared to.

Ought To

Should does not have to be followed by an infinitive: "Harvey should not go, but Martin should be there."

Unfortunately, some writers—and speakers, for that matter—use *ought* in the same way, perhaps savoring the British flavor they think it gives to their sentences, as in, "The court ought not consider that point at all." Sometimes the more literate the writer, the more frequent the error, especially following a negative. Whether the negative or the positive, we *ought to* employ the full infinitive every time:

> "If we press our case, as we ought [read *ought to*], we will have done our client no disservice."

Content/Contents

Do we speak properly of the *content* of a letter or of its *contents*, especially if the letter is long and full of things?

That which is contained in writing is more properly spoken of as *content*. Even if a letter *is* full of things, we will refer to its *content*, singular.

Contents is properly used to mean something tangible, like juice in a bottle or sardines in a can.

Contents should not be used of people or animals—it is better to speak of a car's having disgorged its passengers or occupants, not its contents.

Probably or Likely?

One wonders why otherwise conservative, careful lawyers choose to mess about with the troublesome *likely* when dependable, serviceable, plain old *probably* is just dying for a date. We should not write "Jones will likely refuse our offer" when we can as easily write "Jones will probably refuse our offer."

Likely used as an adjective is just fine: "A recession is likely," or "The plaza site is a likely choice," or "That's a likely story."

Forecast

Forecast is frequently misused (instead of the more usual *predict* or *expect*):

> "Wearing team colors and symbols may be forecast [read *expected*] to cause disruption."

Forecasting is better left to meteorologists.

May/Might

Writers increasingly use these words somewhat whimsically, as in this example:

> "Officer Shear believed the owner may have made an honest mistake when he put the rear license plate on the car, or someone might have been trying to avoid paying a registration fee for an unlicensed vehicle, or the car may have been stolen."

May and *might* are alike in meaning (possibility and permission), but they differ in intensity. Although *might* is the past tense of *may*, both are capable of expressing present and future time. *May* is stronger in both: "She may appear" is stronger than "She might appear." "May I see that?" is stronger than "Might I see that?" *Might* is also useful if we wish to scold mildly: "You might at least look happy about it." *Might*, in the past perfect, sometimes indicates a condition contrary to fact: "They might have won the game, if they had put some effort into it." [But they didn't.]

Grammar seems to take a back seat when *may* or *might* is at the wheel. Although we correctly observe consistency of tense in writing, "He says he may abstain from voting," and "He said he might abstain from voting," we also go beyond the mere grammatical distinction to signify a distinction in meaning, thus apparently mixing the tenses:

> "Any law firm that involves itself too enthusiastically in local elections may lose clients and, depending on the atmosphere at City Hall, might find itself practicing defensive politics instead of practicing law."

No grammatical difference dictates the use here of *may* in one instance and *might* in the other; it is rather that the latter possibility (practicing defensive politics) seems more remote than the former (losing clients).

However

Miss Grammar would like to discourage the ubiquitous use of *however* when a comma and *but* would work much better. For example:

> "It is true that in that panel decision the words 'governmental function' appear. However, the phrase is inapplicable to the decision."
>
> *Better*: "It is true that in that panel decision the words 'governmental function' appear, but the phrase is inapplicable to the decision."

Unfortunately, we see *however* sprinkled on pages like dots on dice. Be especially wary of *however* at the beginning of a sentence, generally the very worst place for the word to be because it is seldom used correctly in that position. At the beginning of a sentence, *however* has far too much contrastive power and may produce an unintended and unwanted comparison with the entire preceding sentence. Do not overlook the beautiful simplicity and clarity of *but*.

Big Words, Wrong Words

One of the countless deadly (or at least ugly) sins in writing is choosing a big, important word when a small, simple one would do the job better. Let's take just a few common offenders.

Obtain

Not only is it harder to say than *get* or *find*, it is also too heavy a word in most cases.

> "Please obtain [get] a copy of this case before our meeting."
>
> "After searching all morning, Ms. Nolan obtained [found] the affidavit."

Fortuitous, Portend, and Enormity

Sometimes words lead us astray—or our assumptions do. *Costive* does not mean "expensive," and you can't play a tune on a *scramasax*.

Fortuitous, regardless of its looks, does not mean "fortunate," "lucky," or "timely." It means occurring by chance—no more, no less, much like *accidentally*.

Portend means to foretell or foreshadow, and it has negative connotations, rather like *bodes* ("His proposal bodes no good"; "His proposal portends disaster for our company"). *Portends* does not make a good substitute for *means*. Related to *portend* is *portentous*, meaning foreboding and ominous. Miss Grammar mentions it only because she is tired of hearing it mispronounced as por-TEN-shus or por-TEN-chew-us.

Enormity does not mean "really big." It means "absolutely awful." We would not want to mistakenly praise the enormity of a contribution or marvel at the *enormity* of Alaska compared with little Rhode Island.

Feelings

"We all do no end of feeling, and we mistake it for thinking." *Mark Twain.*

In Miss G.'s experience, we also do no end of writing the word *feeling* when we mean *thinking* or *believing*, as in:

> "I feel that to pursue the issue of bifurcation would only further alienate the court."

The writer would have done better to *think*, *believe*, *maintain*, or *submit*. He might also have simply said:

> "To pursue this issue of bifurcation would only further alienate the court."

One may feel dizzy, sad, or foolish, but one may not *feel* one's ideas, unless a very careful distinction is made, as in:

> "I have no hard evidence and no recent provocation for believing Jones to be a crook, but I just feel that he is not what he holds himself out to be."

Nauseous/Nauseated

If your client is *nauseated*, he feels sick; if he is *nauseous*, he makes others sick.

Preventive/Preventative

Choose *preventive*; the reason becomes clear from the following example:

> "An ounce of *preventation* is worth a pound of cure."

i.e. and *e.g.*

The meaning of *i.e.* (id est) is "that is"; *e.g.* (exempli gratia) means "for example." If one is uncertain about which one to use, substituting the English meaning may help.

Further, *i.e.* may explain, in the sense of "that is to say" or "in other words"; in addition, it frequently provides a definition of sorts of the *one thing* that has just been mentioned. *E.g.* provides a few items out of *many things* that might be mentioned.

Affect/Effect

Miss Grammar has received a number of inquiries about *affect* and *effect*. The problem seems to center on the verb *affect* and the noun *effect* (*affect* is sometimes a noun, and *effect* is sometimes a verb, which further confuses things).

Generally, to *affect* is to have an influence on, to bring about a change.

> "Being robbed affected Mr. Jones deeply."
> "What was the effect of the robbery on Mr. Jones?"

When used as a verb, to *effect* means to bring about or accomplish.

> "The project was designed to effect savings."

No wonder people would rather use *impact*.

Forgo/Forego, and Other Pairs

It is confusing to deal with pairs of words like *forgo/forego, therefor/therefore,* and *forbear/forebear.* Our greatest aid is the dictionary.

Foregoing means something just past or previously said or written; *forgoing* means abandoning, giving up, or forsaking something.

Similarly, *therefor* means "for that, this, or it," but *therefore* means "hence, for that reason." *Forbear* means to stop doing something; a *forebear* is one's ancestor.

Presently and *Currently*

Currently means "belonging to the present time"; *presently* is now used primarily in the sense of "soon."

Presently meant "immediately" in Shakespeare's day; then its meaning changed to "after a little while" ("He will be here presently"). *Presently* as a synonym for *now* is increasingly used, but the careful, conservative writer will choose *now* or *currently* and avoid the ambiguity.

Lend Me Your Ears

Lend is considered preferable to *loan,* particularly in formal writing: "The bank was not eager to lend the money to Acme Construction." (Past tense *lent*; past participle *has lent*.)

Loan is better saved for use as a noun: "He could not repay the loan."

Assure, Ensure, and Insure

All three mean to make sure or certain.

Assure refers to people and means to set someone's mind at rest: "I assured him of my good intentions."

Insure, like *assure*, has a special meaning of its own—it should be reserved for the sense of guaranteeing something against loss, as with an insurance policy.

In the following sentence, *assure* is misused (a common error, incidentally):

> "This plan will assure [read *ensure*] that the bank will recoup its losses."

Correct use of *assure*:

> "This plan will assure the bank that it will recoup its losses."

Assure is much like *reassure*—there's always someone on the receiving end.

Guaranty and Guarantee

The puzzlement about which of the two spellings, *guarantee* or *guaranty*, is appropriate is easily solved. *Guarantee* may be used in any context and may safely serve as both a verb and a noun: "We guarantee our product, and we put our guarantee in writing."

But *guarantee* may present a problem because proper names of some companies include the word *guaranty*. Also, documents entitled *guaranties* are seen often in our daily work.

Although *guaranty*, too, has served in both capacities—as a verb and as a noun—established business usage has virtually eliminated any verbal function. The contract that *guarantees* the quality of service of a product is, in the world of commerce, the *guaranty*. But apart from this specialized business use, *guaranty* and *guarantee*, as previously pointed out, are interchangeable as nouns. Which term to use, therefore, is simply a matter of personal preference: "The *guaranty* [or *guarantee*] will expire in two months."

Many firms prefer *guaranty* if a noun is required and *guarantee* when a verb is required. Registered trade names are, of course, inviolable, as are preprinted documents.

Anticipate/Expect, Foresee

Rarely is *anticipate* used correctly; if you use the word frequently, you are probably in trouble already.

Anticipate means to do something in advance so as to prevent or forestall: "We anticipated the opposing counsel's motion and filed one of our own."

Also, we can anticipate someone's orders or questions before they are given or posed and—if we are truly brilliant—we can anticipate technological advancements by 20 years with inventions of our own.

Even though dictionaries imply or state directly that *anticipate* may be used as a synonym for *expect*, especially *expect with pleasure*, Miss Grammar sides with Bryan Garner in his classification of that usage as "a slipshod extension" to "be avoided in formal legal writing." *A Dictionary of Modern Legal Usage* 51 (1987).

> *Incorrect*: "Whether that degree of damage could have been anticipated [read *foreseen*] is completely irrelevant."

Incorrect: "We anticipate [read *expect*] that he will be one of the shining stars in the firmament of the partnership."

Such, Said, Same

Such used in place of a regular pronoun is not acceptable to careful writers. It is as common and unattractive as its shabby mates, *said* and *same*. Bryan Garner at page 527 says, "Contrary to what some think, *such* is no more precise than *the*, *that*, or *those*."

In this sentence: "The trustees will have at their disposal when such amendment is made financial data," *such* is to be replaced by *the* (and of course *financial data* must follow *will have*).

Re Same

Have nothing to do with this grubby beast, with or without its *re*. See what a mess it makes:

"Telephone conference with Mr. Jones re stipulated order; conference with Mr. Black re proposed revision; intraoffice conference (Smith/White) re final order and correspondence with Mr. Brown re same."

One probably assumes that *re same* here refers only to the final order, but in this particular instance, all the orders and conferences were the subject of correspondence with Mr. Brown. Instead of *re same*, which is inadequate and misleading, we should write:

"* * * correspondence with Mr. Brown re these orders and conferences."

Same used as a pronoun is considered by Bryan Garner "symptomatic of legalese." There is nothing wrong with the thoughtful repeating of a noun; clarity comes before variety.

In Behalf Of/On Behalf Of

In behalf of means "for the benefit of": "The concert raised thousands of dollars in behalf of unwed grammarians."

On behalf of means "in place of": "Geraldo will speak on behalf of his absent brother."

How to keep them straight? We can memorize these short phrases:

> *In* behalf of: *in* the *interest* of;
>
> *On* behalf of: *on* the part of.

Behalf doesn't comfortably take a plural—beware of such constructions as:

> "We will execute the lease on the behalves of both Hurd and Sweeney."
>
> "Simon and Emily wanted to express their gratitude for your having spoken on his and her behalves."

Compare To/Compare With

Think about this pair for too long and you'll find yourself in the ditch of indecision.

Compare to is used to point out likenesses only: "We can compare his career to an elevator ride, full of ups, downs, and full stops."

Compare with is used when we examine similarities or differences: "Compared with the help he gave to the defendants, his lending me this memorandum is nothing."

Does that mean we can forget *compare to* and just rely on *compare with*? Not really—*compare to* indicates that one has pretty much made up one's mind about the two things in question, while there may be a tentativeness in *compare with*; there is something yet to be decided:

> "The doctor compared the claimant's suicide attempt to sending a telegram for help."
>
> "We can easily compare his objectives with his results."

Compare with is used much more often than *compare to*, probably a reflection of life's own tentativeness.

Absent Without Leave

absent; adjective. Missing or not present. Not existent; lacking. Inattentive.

That's what one finds in most dictionaries, including Black's Law Dictionary. Why, then, do we daily write and read this sort of thing?

> "Absent any other evidence, innocence is clearly established."

Is this legitimate?

If you can find a dictionary that gives *absent* full attention, it will tell you that the word is indeed an adjective, but also a transitive verb ("He absented himself from the room") and a preposition. Yes, a preposition, according to Webster's Third unabridged, no matter how many of William Safire's readers have written abusive and scolding letters to the contrary (*I Stand Corrected* 284-87 (1984)). Safire himself believes "the vogue use of *absent* as a preposition" is sure to draw the fire of a "jargon-hater."

Absent functions nicely as a preposition, as does its cousin *without*; the meanings are similar too. So why do we need *absent*? Probably because *without* has other, unrelated meanings and because there are subtle differences:

"Without a doubt, he is guilty" is different from "absent a doubt"—something we would not say.

Absent strongly suggests *if*, finishing up with a prediction, but *without* does not:

> "Absent a firm understanding of the situation, he will fail."
> ["If he does not understand * * *."]

> "Without a firm understanding of the situation, he entered the judge's chambers."
> [He did not understand.]

William Safire may be quite right when he declares that *absent* is "all over the public prints"; in the past ten years Miss Grammar has seen two other previously "legal-only" expressions snatched up by the admiring public: *at risk*, meaning "in danger," and *expose*, meaning "to put someone or something in a perilous position." Those who dislike the sound of *absent* can achieve the same result with "in the absence of."

16

MISCELLANY

These two columns defy classification, but Miss Grammar includes them because they have been among the most popular of all those printed.

The Becky Klemt Letter

A few years ago, Becky Klemt, a lawyer in Laramie, Wyoming, wrote a letter—and *what* a letter! It has become "the most photocopied letter in legal history," according to *The Wall Street Journal* (Sept. 6, 1990), and Miss Grammar thinks the complete set of correspondence is worthy of reprinting here.

The First Letter

Mr. Stephen G. Corris
Attorney at Law
Irvine, California 16424

Dear Mr. Corris:

This firm obtained the enclosed Judgment against Defendant Stephen H. Broomell, on June 4, 1987.

The Judgment remains only partially satisfied, and there is due and owing as of this date principal and interest in the amount of $4,239.84. Interest accrues at the rate of $1.06 per day.

Would you please advise whether or not you would be interested in collecting on this Judgment and, if so, your fees for doing so. It's entirely possible that a letter from you to Mr. Broomell will be all that's needed.

I look forward to hearing from you.

Sincerely,
Pence and MacMillan
Becky N. Klemt

The Second Letter (Corris's reply)

Dear Ms. Klemt,

I apologize for not getting back to you sooner, but I have been in and out of the office for the past six weeks. Seems that there's never enough time.

I want to thank you for offering me the opportunity to collect the judgment on behalf of Ms. Marcia L. Broomell, but, I must decline.

Without sounding pretentious, my current retainer for cases is a flat $100,000, with an additional charge of $1,000 per hour. Since I specialize in international trade and geopolitical relations between the Middle East and Europe, my clientele is very unique and limited, and I am afraid I am unable to accept other work at this time.

I am enclosing the copy you sent of the judgment and again, Ms. Klemt, I thank you for your thoughts. It was very nice of you.

Very sincerely,
Stephen G. Corris

The Third Letter (The potshot heard around the world)

Dear Steve:

I am in receipt of your letter to me dated August 8, 1988, regarding collection of a judgment against Stephen Broomell.

Steve, I've got news—you can't say you charge a $100,000 retainer fee and an additional $1,000 an hour without sounding pretentious. It just can't be done. Especially when you're writing to someone in Laramie, Wyoming, where you're considered pretentious if you wear socks to Court or drive anything fancier than a Ford Bronco. Hell, Steve, all the lawyers in Laramie, put together, don't charge $1,000 an hour.

Anyway, we were sitting around the office discussing your letter and decided that you had a good thing going. We doubt we could get away with charging $1,000 an hour in Laramie (where people are more inclined to barter with livestock than pay in cash), but we do believe we could join you in California, where evidently people can get away with just about anything. Therefore, the four lawyers in our firm intend to join you in the practice of international trade and geopolitical relations between the Middle East and Europe.

Now, Steve, you're probably thinking that we don't know anything about the Middle East and Europe, but I think you'll be pleasantly surprised to find that this is not the case. Paul Schierer is actually from the Middle East—he was raised outside of Chicago, Illinois, and although those national newsmen insist on calling Illinois the Midwest, to us, if it's between New York and the Missouri River, it's the Middle East.

Additionally, although I have never personally been to Europe myself, my sister just returned from a vacation there and told me lots about it, so I believe I would be of some help to you on that end of the negotiations. Hoke MacMillan has actually been there, although it was 15 years ago, so you might have to update him on recent geopolitical developments. Also, Hoke has applied to the Rotary Foreign Exchange Program for a 16-year-old Swedish girl and believes she will be helpful in preparing him for trips abroad.

Another thing you should know, Steve, is that the firm has an extensive foreign language background, which I believe would be useful to you. Hoke took Latin in high school, although he hasn't used it much, inasmuch as he did not become a pharmacist or a priest. Vonnie Nagel took high school German, while Paul has eaten in Italian restaurants. I, myself, majored in French in college, until I realized that probably wasn't the smartest career move in the world. I've forgotten such words as "international" and "geopolitical" (which I'm not too familiar with in English), but I can still hail a taxi or find a restroom, which might come in handy.

Steve, let us know when we should join you in California so that we can begin doing whatever it is you do. In anticipation of our move, we've all been practicing trying to say we charge $1,000 an hour with a straight face, but so far, we haven't been able to do it. I suspect it'll be easier once we actually reach California where I understand they charge $5,000,000 for one-bedroom condos and everybody (even poor people) drives a Mercedes. Anyway, because I'll be new to the area of international trade and geopolitical relations, I'm thinking of charging only $500-$600 an hour to begin with. Will that be enough to meet our overhead?

I look forward to hearing from you before you go away again for six weeks.

Sincerely,
Becky Klemt

> P.S. Incidentally, we have advised our client of your hourly rate. She is willing to pay you $1,000 per hour to collect this judgment provided it doesn't take you more than four seconds.

Poor Stephen G. Corris, "the butt of a thousand faxes," says his "usual charge is closer to $500 per hour. 'I got calls from one Washington firm and two in New York,' he says, 'basically asking, How are you pulling this off? They wanted a piece of my action. I said get lost.' "

Poor Ms. Broomell says: "Sure, sure, it's all incredible. Now a thousand lawyers know about my plight, and not one of them can be bothered to collect my money!"

A Grammatical Exchange

Among Miss Grammar's acquaintances is the excellent grammarian Robert C. Cumbow, of Seattle. Miss G. was so amused by his recent letter that she thought it worthwhile to print part of the recent correspondence:

Dear Bob,

What do you think of "outsourcing," as in:

> "Restructuring and reorganizing the office workspace has been a common response, resulting in downsizing, rightsizing, redeployment—and outsourcing."

This pearl is from John B. Dykeman, writing in *Modern Office Technology*, October 1991, p. 10.

What means this outsourcing, you ask? The farming out of in-house functions, like photocopying or graphic arts.

On to another matter:

During the last few years, I have read of poor souls who needed to be shrouded in straightjackets, evidently having found themselves in dire straights or straightened circumstances—perhaps because their straight-laced Great Aunt Tillie, who had drowned in the Straight of Juan de Fuca, had left her fortune to charity.

As Great Aunt Tillie used to say to her infamous Persian cat from hell, "No, no, Fluffy!" There is a difference between *straight* and *strait*, and that difference is worth knowing. In all the usages in the preceding paragraph, the spelling should have been accomplished without the *gh*: straitjacket, dire straits, straitened circumstances, strait-laced, and Strait. The meaning to be conveyed is not "extending continuously in the same direction without curving (straight)," but "narrow or constricted (strait)."

I am surprised to learn that the rock group, Dire Straits, has selected the proper spelling, especially in view of the liberties that Mötley Crüe and Def Leppard have taken.

Even Holy writ gets savaged: writers should watch out for Matthew 7:14 (some lawyers of my acquaintance quote Scripture constantly): it's *strait*: "Because strait is the gate, and narrow is the way which leadeth unto life . . . ." Sort of like the entrance unto Grammarland.

—Karen

Dear Karen,

I join you in hating "outsourcing." I'm not categorically opposed to verbing the noun, or to neologisms that are useful,
sensible, and necessary. But outsourcing? It doesn't say what it
means, *or* mean what it says! Who would ever dream that it refers
to what the rest of us have always called "farming out" or "going
outside" (as in, "we'll do this one in house, but we'll go outside for
that one")?

You shouldn't be surprised at the literacy of Dire Straits.
They're a good group, with about 15 years of well-written string-
band, jazz-influenced rock behind them. Their lead singer, gui-
tarist, and composer is Mark Knopfler, whose refinement is
apparent from the fact that he wrote the lovely, lovely score for
the lovely, lovely film *Local Hero*.

Dire Straits doesn't deserve to be mentioned in the same
paragraph as Mötley Crüe and Def Leppard, which are heavy-
metal groups. The name of the former, by the way, exemplifies
one of my pettest of peeves: the use of a diacritical mark as if it
were a decoration rather than part of the spelling of the word.
The letter combination "üe," besides being unpronounceable,
doesn't appear in any known language; and in most languages
that use an umlaut, "ü" and "ue" are interchangeable. I wrote to
Eugene Maleska once when his New York Times crossword
puzzle gave "Die Zauberflote" as the answer to a clue about a
Mozart opera. I told him that I recognized the difficulty in putting
"Die Zauberflöte" into a crossword grid, but what was the problem with "Die Zauberfloete"? I told him that one can't simply
dispense with an inconvenient diacritical mark, any more than
one can arbitrarily cast a letter out of a word. I gave as an
example the blunder that *Games* magazine made when they gave
"ano" as the answer to a clue that called for the Spanish word for
"year." A Spanish-speaking reader had to educate them that "año"
means year and "ano" is where the sun don't shine. I got back

from Maleska one of the rudest letters I've ever received from a public personage whom I had theretofore rather liked, telling me that I knew nothing of the challenges and travails of making crosswords and generally inviting me to shut up. Now every Sunday when I do the NYT crossword I think of that letter and mutter to myself. If I had any real gumption I'd stop doing it altogether, but I love it so much (the puzzle, not the muttering). Still, I'll love it more when Maleska isn't editing it any longer. Strait, indeed, is the gate.

—Bob

INDEX

An Informal Bibliography

For general office use, you probably will find William A. Sabin's *The Gregg Reference Manual* (7th ed 1992) to be a real help. Miss Grammar has also included here her opinions about other books that she uses every day.

1. American Heritage Dictionary of the English Language (3d ed 1992).

   —Its usage notes are very valuable.

2. A Dictionary of Modern English Usage, H. W. Fowler (2d ed 1965).

   —Grammar for the purist and the scholar; probably boring and esoteric for others.

3. A Dictionary of Modern Legal Usage, B. Garner (1987).

   —The last word in usage; intelligent and humorous.

4. Drafting Legal Documents, B. Child (West 1988).

   —Wonderful. You can't afford to leave home without this one.

5. The Elements of Legal Style, B. Garner (1991).

   —Excellent.

6. The Grammatical Lawyer, M. S. Freeman (1979).

   —A compilation of old columns—occasionally helpful.

7. Hodges' Harbrace College Handbook (9th ed 1984).

    —Actually, any edition is useful. Good, plain, everyday grammar.

8. Legal Writing: Sense and Nonsense, D. Mellinkoff (1982).

    —Take this with a grain of salt—he's impatient and reckless.

9. Style, Ten Lessons in Clarity and Grace, J. Williams (1981).

    —Great study of noun-heavy sentences. The first edition is far superior to the "improved" edition.